T0095951

The Nathan Roberts House as it appeared circa 1896, located on the old Seneca Turn-pike, now New York State Route 5.

NATHAN ROBERTS

DORRIS MOORE LAWSON

EDITED BY

ERIC W. LAWSON, SR.

NATHAN ROBERTS

ISBN 0-925168-57-2

Cover: Portrait of Nathan Roberts by William Henry Dorance.
Courtesy of the New York State Museum — 55.51

Library of Congress Cataloging-in-Publication Data

In Progress.

North Country Books, Inc.
311 Turner Street
Utica, New York 13501

To the memory of
Dr. Robert Rayback
Professor Emeritus of History
Syracuse University

Bob was Dorris' professor of history and
guided her first effort in biographical
research. He was also a faculty
colleague of mine and
a good friend to both of us.

CONTENTS

Preface

My wife, Dorris, and I became interested in Nathan Roberts soon after we purchased and began renovating a house in Canastota, New York which was known then—but not by us—as the Nathan Roberts House. Renovation became our number one priority. At first that consisted of making it habitable—a new furnace and storm windows for example. Later we would turn to such things as fresh wallpaper and landscaping. The last phase of the project is still under way. As I write this, the dining room floor is emerging from the wall-to-wall rug under which its defects were hidden for over forty years. A natural finished oak floor with an Oriental rug is my current objective.

We discovered by chance that this house was listed in "The Great Georgian Houses of America." We had been told that Roberts was "some kind" of an engineer on the Erie Canal. Gradually, in reading a few items and by hearsay, we began to realize that Roberts was a man of some unusual abilities who had done more than just build a beautiful house and survey the route of the Erie.

Dorris held a master's degree in History from Syracuse University, having written as her thesis a biography of Mary Walker of Oswego, a doctor in the U.S. Army during the Civil War. Her instincts as a historian were whetted by the fact that she was a history teacher—sometimes called a social studies teacher—in the local high school. She first wrote a pamphlet called "Italians in Canastota." And in response to an expressed curriculum need, she then wrote a "History of Canastota." Dorris was the instigator of our project. She discovered what could be found out about Roberts—over and beyond the piece in the Dictionary of American Biography.

While I was not directly involved with Dorris' previous projects, I was interested in Nathan Roberts. At first I did a small amount of research and made some writing suggestions. Eventually I supplied some extensive editorial changes and rewrote several passages. One of these research endeavors was quite fruitless, but interesting just the same. Roberts spent the last two or three years of his Erie experience designing the locks in western New York which carried the Erie up and /or down the rock escarpment over which Niagara Falls tumbled some twenty miles to the west. He subsequently supervised the building of the locks at a spot which became known as Lockport.

It appeared obvious to us that, with a person of Roberts' accomplishments in residence at the start of a new enterprise and the beginning of a new municipality, there would be a treasure trove of material about him in the local library. It fell to me to investigate and report on this source.

Unfortunately, our time in the Lockport public library turned up a lot of material on the in-fighting which accompanied the bringing of a water supply to the area. The real estate and political battles were documented copiously but we could find nothing on the man, Roberts, who lived in the community for an extended period and was the person in charge of transforming a wilderness spot into a beehive of activity. In any event we spent no more time in Lockport.

It is possible that Roberts' nature was a problem in doing research on his life and activities. He went about his tasks in a quiet, reserved manner and did not seek publicity. In fact, late in his career he discovered that meritocracy did not always carry the day. He had been engaged to carry out the widening of the Erie in the late 1840's. He had a worldwide reputation as a canal engineer and an enviable string of accomplishments behind him. Despite these credentials, he lost his position because of a shift of political power in Albany.

Fortunately, as the text shows, there were other sources of information such as newspapers, books, and official reports. One source was particularly helpful and merits some special attention.

Dorris was Historian for the Town of Lenox and, as such, she knew quite a few of the historians of the surrounding towns. Their meetings, chance or otherwise, proved quite helpful at times. Through one of these historians she learned that a lady in Cazenovia had a manuscript that related to Nathan Roberts.

The Cazenovia lady was contacted immediately. She was the widow of a man who was quite an enthusiastic local history buff. She had in her possession a memento, a document which her husband had typed from a handwritten record kept by Nathan Roberts of his daily activities. The lady was not at all interested in the document except as a keepsake as she had no interest in history, local or otherwise. She had no knowledge of where her husband had acquired temporary possession of the journal nor did she know what had happened to it after it had been copied. She was willing for it to be used by Dorris as long as it was returned.

This document was the source for many of the text references to events not otherwise recorded. I was casually aware of this document at the time Dorris had it, but I made no record of the matter and know no more than related here. The document was returned as promised, but unfortunately I do not even know the lady's name.

An editorial note about style is warranted. When Dorris was writing her master's thesis about Mary Walker, she was encouraged by her advisor to brighten up some passages with statements that could not be verified. These fictive touches did not alter known facts or supply crucial matter. An example would be the characterization of a day as rainy or hot, even though there was no record available about the weather for that day and place.

Dorris used this device sparingly in her thesis. Even so, she received some comments from other members of her examining committee even though they was enthusiastic about her paper. She has used it in her short histories about people and events in Canastota. She has used it in this text in a limited way. I do not think that it detracts from the more factual account which constitutes the bulk of the story.

In a way there is a kind of circumstantial evidence to support such statements as in the first chapter. Thus, it is known that Roberts spent a certain summer in Maine. He was poor and did not own a horse, therefore he had to walk to get there. It can be assumed that there were some warm or even hot days during that summer. So it is not unreasonable to say that at the end of one such day he was tired and sweaty with sore feet.

The benefit is that Nathan is presented as a human being rather than as a superman destined to perform unusual feats. The record shows that much later in life he rode a horse all the way from Muscle Shoals in Tennessee to Canastota in a relatively short time. This was a physical feat of remarkable proportions for an elderly person, but it was in keeping with the activity of a person who at an early age had walked from New Jersey to Maine during a hot summer.

There is some confusion in some people's minds about what is meant by the title "Erie Canal." The original Erie, the one Nathan Roberts contributed so much to, was superseded in 1918 by what is properly known as the New York State Barge Canal. The latter is often referred to as the Erie Canal because of several similarities.

When the Barge Canal was opened in 1918, much of the old Erie was abandoned altogether. Other parts were converted to the Barge Canal, as was true for the stretch between Lockport and the Buffalo harbor. Other stretches were left with operating levels of water and partially integrated with the natural drainage system. The stretch between the "wide waters" just east of DeWitt to Rome in an example of the latter treatment. That stretch is used by canoers and other boaters for recreation purposes. For most of that distance the state maintains a towpath for use of pedestrians and bike riders; it is one of the longest and narrowest parks in existence.

The basic reason for the relocation and renovation of the canal was the ability to use natural waterways, such as the Mohawk River and Oneida Lake. The advent of mechanical methods of locomotion for the barges, tugs and other boats meant that towpaths for the horses and mules were no longer needed.

The state still owns the two waterways, maintaining the channel and locks used by the Barge Canal. For a good many years the Barge Canal was a major avenue for moving freight. That use has diminished. The management of the system is now in the hands of the Thruway Authority. Traffic on the Barge Canal is now recreational. The freight that once would travel by boat now has the option of truck or train transportation. The Welland Canal and the Seaway development of the St. Lawrence River, of course, make possible the use of ocean-going freighters for mid-west traffic.

The Barge Canal uses a larger and longer lock system at Lockport than Roberts constructed, but remnants of Roberts' creation can still be seen. For a person who is interested in fine stonework, these relics reward inspection.

1

Nathan S. Roberts

The young man wearily pulled the oxen to the side of the road. He sat down on the grassy bank and pushed the sweat-soaked blonde hair out of his eyes. He was so exhausted, and still the sun beat down unmercifully, and it would be hours before the cool evening would bring relief. His feet, blistered from pebbles which had worked their way into his boots, throbbed and burned.

Perhaps it had been a mistake to bring the oxen. On his previous trips without the team, he had made good time by hitching rides with passing wagons. He knew, however, that the oxen would be of invaluable help when he arrived at Moretown. Even so, had he not been seventeen years old and considered to be a man, and had he not have been of stoic Pilgrim ancestry, he might have cried from fatigue and frustration.

Before he opened his pack, he knew it contained only a partial loaf of stale bread and that his canteen was nearly empty; however, this bare fare would have to serve as lunch as he had not seen a house for miles. People along the way had been kind, giving him bed and board even when they had little. Conversation and news of the outside world was all the thanks they wanted. Many had heard of his grandfather, John Roberts, who had been killed in the French and Indian War in 1764 while serving under Sir William Pepperal. John had left his wife to bring up the children including Abraham, Nathan's father.

As Nathan rested, his mind reverted to his home life in Piles Grove, New Jersey. As he thought of the grinding poverty at home and of the hard work his mother had to do in caring for his brothers and sisters, his jaw hardened in determination that it would not always be so. He did not really blame his father who seemed to be the victim of hard luck. Abraham had found life tilling the soil of New Hampshire less than satisfying, so being of an adventurous nature, he left for the West Indies to seek his fortune. He became quite prosperous there, but when America began its protestations against England prior to the Declaration of Independence, he decided to return to his native land. Unfortunately he was captured by a British cruiser and thus lost his freedom and his fortune. He was forced

1

to serve in several engagements against his country. Somehow, he escaped and settled in the township of Piles Grove, New Jersey where on July 28, 1776, Nathan Smith Roberts was born. Abraham Roberts' experiences in captivity left him in ill health and devoid of the ambition which had propelled him to the West Indies.

Nathan carried his precious math books in his pack. The year before, when only sixteen, he had taught school in Plainfield, New Jersey near the Meridian meeting house; however, with only a common school education, he doubted seriously his ability to teach. Mathematics fascinated him, and he determined to study at night learning all he could, both for himself and for his students. How he wished he could attend either Princeton or the University of Pennsylvania, both near his home but both beyond his financial reach.

With money earned from his first teaching job, he purchased one hundred acres of land at two dollars an acre at Moretown, Vermont, ten miles west of Montpelier, three hundred miles from his home in Piles Grove. This land was his destination when we find him beside the road.

During that summer, Nathan chopped several acres of heavy timber and worked part time for a Captain Morgan by whom he was paid sixteen dollars. In the fall he sold the land at a profit and returned to Plainfield to teach again at a salary of ten dollars a month.

For a number of years, the pattern of Roberts' life was pretty much the same, teaching in the winter and land speculating or working on the land in summer.

In 1799, he taught at Boscaneau for the same salary, ten dollars a month. This was the year of the death of George Washington whom Roberts admired greatly. He organized a solemn ceremony to honor the country's greatest leader.

In most of Nathan Roberts' real estate dealings, he made a profit; however, in the spring of 1800, he purchased two hundred acres of land for four hundred twenty dollars from Timothy Hinman in Denby, Vermont. This turned out to be a bad investment, since the title was not clear. Sixteen years later, it was necessary for Roberts to pay Isaac Beers of New haven, Connecticut one hundred fifty dollars to clear the title.

During the winters of 1801 and 1802, Roberts returned to his teaching post at Plainfield; however, in the summer of 1801, he once again went land speculating in Vermont where he bought one hundred eighty acres in the Town of Huntsburg on the east side of the pond at five dollars an acre. During the summer, he cleared fourteen acres of this land, and in the fall exchanged the land for six hundred acres in Compton in lower Canada.

Discouraged by the continuing low salaries for teachers, he decided to spend the winter of 1803 in land speculation. He examined lands in the Black River area of New York State, land which he had bought but had never seen. At the end of the winter, after several purchases, sales and trades, he ended up with a farm in Watertown, New York.

The lure of academic life was strong for Nathan Roberts. He missed his pupils and his teaching. Somewhere in his travels, he met Ansel White who, without too much pressure, persuaded Roberts to teach in Oriskany, New York. Ansel White was the son of Hugh White, first settler of the town which bears his name, in fact the first white settler in the Utica area of New York. Ansel had heard of Roberts' reputation as a good teacher and sent his three children to Roberts' school. The children were Ebenezer, Aurchia, and Lavinia, eleven years old at this time. Little did Nathan imagine that many years later, Lavinia would become his wife. White persuaded Roberts to move to Whitestown to teach for the next two years. He did, however, do some surveying to eke out his salary. This experience was to stand him in good stead later.

In 1806, a Dr. Shaw talked Roberts into teaching at Westmoreland. In June of that year, there was a total eclipse of the sun which impressed Roberts' greatly. As he described it, "It was of two hours duration—from 1 o'clock to 3 o'clock p.m. fowls went to roost, cattle also. The earth appeared clouded with twilight. There was a cold chill as of evening and the stars were visible."

Once more Ansel White talked Roberts into teaching at Whitesboro and he remained there through 1809. The school had become so large by this time that it had to be divided. Roberts' salary had increased to sixteen dollars a month plus subsistence. From time to time during this period, he took trips to his farm on the Black River. He had cleared fifty acres and had built a house and barn there. He probably intended to make this his home someday; however, in 1809, Mr. More offered him two thousand dollars for the farm. Such an offer was too good to refuse, so he sold.

His next job was as an assistant teacher at the Fairfield Academy in Herkimer County. The Reverend Caleb Alexander was the preceptor. Roberts' salary was only sixty dollars a quarter and board; however, here he had the advantage of taking courses in chemistry, anatomy and surgery under Professors Noyes and Jacobs. To one of Roberts' intellectual curiosity, the courses were well worth the slight reduction in pay.

Still, he had not decided what to do with his life. He was now thirty-four years old and was still searching, supporting himself on low teachers' pay and a bit of land speculation. This was a far cry from accomplishing his goal of escaping poverty, so in 1810, he decided to go west. He only got as far as Chautauqua, New York, where he took a fancy to a tract of land owned by Captain McClentock. He paid fourteen hundred dollars for one hundred forty acres, forty of which were cleared and on which there was a house of logs.

Once again in July, we find him back teaching at Whitesboro but still disconnected with his life. During that winter, he decided to investigate the mercantile life. He hired a substitute for ten days and went with William B. Savage to the falls of the Genesee where Rochester now stands. He had thought that perhaps this would be a good spot on which to locate a tavern or store; however, on arrival, he found only a wilderness with the exception of one house and an old mill, hardly a place in which business would flourish. Discouraged, he returned to his teaching job at Whitesboro.

His dream of a business career was not dead. The next year, 1811, he was engaged as overseer and clerk in the Oneida Manufacturing Society, a cotton factory, at a salary of ten shillings a day. This cotton factory was the first one built west of Cooperstown. Roberts was employed here for about three years keeping accounts and selling goods to agents. Business was unusually profitable, as this was the period of the Embargo Act and the non-intercourse laws. While working at the factory, Roberts bought a large farm in the Town of Lenox, Madison County, for five thousand dollars for which he had to go in debt. He also put three hundred sheep, which cost seven hundred dollars, and a considerable number of cows and horses on the farm. He hired a local man, Mr. Butler, to tend the farm. The price of wool fell and the value of the sheep declined. In addition to the farm debt, a Dr. Capron, who owed Roberts twelve hundred dollars, failed. It took his son, N.J. Capon, four years to repay Roberts. Because of these transactions, we find Roberts not only not well-to-do but deeply in debt. The sixteen hundred dollars which he received for the sale of his Chautauqua property and which he invested in the factory made hardly a dent in his bills.

By 1814, he had become dissatisfied with his job, which was not surprising, for the work was dull and monotonous. He sold out his interest in the business for twenty-one hundred dollars and moved near Whitmore to teach. His stay here was very short-lived, because as soon as it was known that Roberts was again teaching, he was once again invited to become head of the Academy in Whitesboro. He only stayed in this job for the year at the end of which Mr. Wolcott offered Roberts a job as head of the Whitestown Cotton Factory for three years at two dollars a day. This was a considerable raise in pay, so Roberts accepted. So he vacillated between the love of teaching and the need to succeed financially.

Mercantile ventures were not thriving at this time. As Roberts wrote in 1816,

> "This year the manufacturing of cotton, etc. was a very dull business. At the close of the war, British cotton goods of all description were imported, so low and the price of the raw material of cotton was so high in England that inevitable ruin seemed to be the impending fate of the American manufacturers in general. The factory in which I was engaged felt those effects very sensibly. Various meetings were called and the stockholders took measures to curtail their business and to reduce their expenses. I proposed to them to allow me wages for one month in advance to close my accounts, and I would give up my agreement. This was agreed to and an amicable settlement was entered into with all parties of the concern. I am happy to say that I have never been called upon to explain or correct any amounts whatever since, although during the five years in which I was engaged in said factories, property to the amount of about two thousand dollars a week passed through my hands as principal clerk and agent. Great sums of this was cash. I closed in May 1816."

So might Nathan Roberts have continued all his life, changing from teaching, to business, to land speculating, but an event in 1816 was to change his life, as well as the lives of may others, dramatically. The Erie Canal was begun! The connection between a teacher in a pioneer Whitestown, a dabbler in land sales, and the huge projected Erie Canal may seem indeed far fetched, but strange things were happening in America at this time.

2

DREAMS

The idea of a canal to join the Atlantic to the Great Lakes was not new. A hundred years before the Erie was built, Cadwallader Colden, a surveyor-general of New York State, had an idea for a canal to ease traffic across the State. Benjamin Franklin dreamed of a similar facility for his state of Pennsylvania. George Washington, after a tour of the Mohawk Valley in 1773, wrote of the possibilities of a canal system linking east to west.

Finally, in 1785, an engineer, Christopher Colles, made a survey of the Mohawk Valley, as far as Fort Stanwix (Rome), noting the obstructions in the river. He proposed seven miles of bypass canals around such problem area as Cohoes Falls, Little Falls, and Fort Schuyler. It was a good plan, but like many good plans, it had to wait its time. It was six years later, in 1791, that the Legislature passed a bill to form two companies to build two canals in two regions of the State. The Western Inland Lock Navigation Company was to join the Hudson to Lake Champlain.

In 1793, a canal to bypass Little Falls was begun. For two years, five hundred men worked on this canal only one mile long. About half the distance was through solid rock. When the canal was finished, the cost was so great that the state had to come to the aid of the company. A canal at Rome to join the upper Mohawk with Wood Creek was also completed; however, the Cohoes project was abandoned as being too expensive. The Northern Inland Lock Navigation Company, with a loss of $100,000, was a financial disaster and accomplished nothing. In 1810, the state finally bought out the companies for $150,000.

In spite of the financial losses, the building of the two canals must be deemed a success. Now Durham boats, carrying loads of ten or eleven tons, could be used in place of the old river bateaux which could carry only one ton. The cost per ton was dramatically reduced from fourteen dollars to five dollars.

This was a beginning, but the need for a complete canal was great. The cost per ton of shipping was one hundred dollars from Lake Erie to New York City. For a person wishing to make the trip west, the journey was time consuming, expensive, and uncomfortable. First the traveler had to take a sailing vessel from New York to Albany which consumed two to five days. This trip was rather pleasant unless one was in a hurry. In Albany, after a delay, he took a coach to Schenectady, a distance of seventeen miles. Here he waited for a boat to transport him one hundred four miles on the Mohawk River which took another week. From Utica to Oswego a combination of land coaches and boats transported the traveler one hundred fourteen miles in a mere eight to ten days. The trip finally ended after a boat trip on Lake Ontario to Lewiston and overland to Buffalo. If one felt a pressing need to go to Buffalo, he knew it would take at least a month. The alternative was a trip by stagecoach, but this was much more uncomfortable and uncertain. Roads at that time were, for the most part, muddy lanes. The improved roads were corduroy, roads made by placing logs side by side and covering them with dirt and stones, hardly a cushioned ride in a coach with inadequate springs. The trip could also be expensive, as nearly all roads were toll roads and privately owned.

In 1806, Jesse Hawley, a flour merchant, came up with the first clear concept of a canal across the State. At the time, Hawley was serving a twenty month sentence in debtors' prison as a result of his partner's financial failure. Hawley wrote a series of fourteen essays which were published in the Genesee Messenger under the pseudonym "Hercules." These essays, widely read, brought to the public the problem and a possible solution. Perhaps, more important, the essays came to the attention of DeWitt Clinton.

DeWitt Clinton was a Johnny-come-lately to speculations concerning a canal, but when his interest was engaged, he became totally involved. DeWitt Clinton was politically the most powerful man in New York State having been a United States Senator, a three-term mayor of New York City and a member of the State Assembly. Thomas Jefferson thought Clinton was the most important man in the United States. Clinton might have become president of the United States but for his untimely death at fifty-nine in 1828. In 1810, his help was solicited by Jonas Platt, a political opponent, on the canal issue. Clinton seconded Platt's resolution to form a Board of Canal Commissioners. The Commission was appointed consisting of Governeur Morris, Stephen Van Rensselaer, Simon Dewitt, William North, Thomas Eddy, Peter Porter, and DeWitt Clinton.

In 1808, Judge James Geddes, lawyer, judge, businessman in the salt industry of Onondaga was appointed by Clinton to make a survey of a possible canal route. Six hundred dollars was approved for the project, which proved insufficient, so Geddes supplemented from his private funds. Geddes studied two routes, one to Lake Ontario, one to Lake Erie. He favored the route to Erie, because he felt that the route to Lake Ontario would lead to traffic on the St. Lawrence, to Canada and thus to the British.

It was still to be eight years before the canal would be started. One obstacle was the enormous amount of money needed for the project which was considered madness by many people of the state; however, with Albert Gallatin's Report on Internal Improvements and with the general prosperity of the country, it was thought that the canal project might be a combination State and Federal undertaking. Judge Asa Forman and William Kirkpatrick, prominent New York legislators, were chosen to visit President Jefferson to request funds. Thomas Jefferson, the most progressive innovator of the time, responded thus:

> "It is a splendid project and may be executed a century hence. Why, Sir, here is a canal of a few miles projected by General Washington which, if completed, would render this a fine commercial city, which has languished for many years because the small sum of $200,000 necessary to complete it cannot be obtained from the federal government or from individuals. And you talk of making a canal 350 miles long through a wilderness! It is little short of madness to think of it at this day!"

But the madness continued. Hundreds of people in eastern New York and in New England waited hopefully for an easier route to western lands where the land was fertile, cheap and free of New England stones. More and more, farmers already in the west, turned to the Mississippi River as a cheaper, safer route on which to send their produce to Europe. New Orleans was becoming a threat to New York City. Jesse Hawley continued his barrage of essays in favor of canal construction. DeWitt Clinton, using his great political clout, finally even got support from his political opponent, Van Buren. All seemed ready, but the War of 1812 had to be fought before domestic progress could begin in earnest.

In the early spring of 1817, DeWitt Clinton promised, "What has been accomplished elsewhere we shall accomplish here; the day will come in less than ten years when we shall see Erie water flowing into the Hudson."

3

LIFE BEGINS AT FORTY

It has been said that life begins at forty. For Nathan Roberts this proved true, for in 1816, two events happened which were to set the course of his life for the next twenty-five years. In June of that year, Judge Benjamin Wright appointed him assistant engineer to explore and survey the route of the Erie Canal from Rome to the Seneca River. Wright had been put in charge of the middle section of the canal. At the time, there were no trained engineers in America as there were no schools of engineering. Wright had a good deal of experience in surveying. In fact, he had been in charge of the first overview of the canal route when the legislature first voted for such a study. He had reported favorably on the prospect of such a canal. When Wright began his search for assistants, he decided on Roberts because of his thorough knowledge of mathematics.

On the first of July, 1816, starting at Rome, Roberts, with thirteen men, began to explore the wilderness to the west. By November first, they had reached Montezuma. The party was lodged in tents at night, and rach morning, they faced the seemingly endless wilderness, the heat and the mosquitoes. The lack of fresh food, unobtainable because of the lack of farms or settlements along the way, was a special hardship. Roberts described the daily menu: "breakfast—chocolate, a piece of pork, salt and hard, hard bread. Dinner: boiled or frizzed pork, hard bread, whiskey and swamp water. Supper: hard bread and milk if we could get it—scarcely any."

On November 4, 1816, there occurred the second event which was to mold Nathan Roberts' life. He described the event in his journal:

> "Married Lavinia White—Monday evening by Reverend John Frost-Whitesborough, know her about ten years, last four years more in particular. In 1804, she attended my school at Oriskany and when I came to Whitesborough, she attended my school more or less for several years. I believe that we are both convinced that the motives which united us have been strengthened by friendship and affectionate regard for each other's welfare and happiness."

Lavinia White was the daughter of Ansel White and granddaughter of Hugh White, founder of Whitesboro, or Whitestown as it was then called. He had been the first white settler in the area and had been extremely successful in dealings with the Indians. The story goes that to demonstrate his trust in the Indians, at one time he allowed them to take his baby granddaughter, Lavinia's sister, to their camp for overnight. She was to be returned at noon the next day. Noon came but no Indians. As the afternoon waned, the prostrate mother collapsed, fearing that her child was dead. At sundown, there appeared on the horizon a contingent of Indians led by the little girl replete with Indian head-dress and robes, on an Indian pony led by the chief.

Lavinia, at the time of her marriage was twenty-four years old and Nathan was sixteen years older. At a time when most girls were married at seventeen or eighteen, Lavinia was a mature woman. Perhaps this accounts for the success of a marriage which must have been strained by Roberts' long absences from home. During these absences, Lavinia had the burden of the management of a large farm, the upbringing of six children, one grandchild and the supervising of the erection of a mansion.

Roberts left Lavinia in Whitesboro at the home of her father almost immediately after the wedding, because he had contracted with Wright to spend the winter in Rome preparing maps. He returned to Whitesboro as often as possible to see Lavinia; however, most of his time was spent in Rome studying as there was much to learn. This time in Rome would have been a lonely time but for the company of a brilliant young relative. Canvass White was planning the Canal east while Roberts planned west.

Canvass White was the most outstanding of Hugh White's grandsons. From infancy, he was a frail and delicate child; notwithstanding, his accomplishments were many.

His childhood was spent on his father's farm where his innovative genius produced a number of improvements in agricultural implements. His early schooling was sporadic because of his health. When he could, he attended Roberts' school.

In 1811 when White was twenty-one, he was sent on a sea voyage to Europe for his health. On the return trip, he was captured by the British, war having been declared between Britain and the United States. He was soon released and, on his return, he entered Fairfield Academy where he completed his education. In 1814 White raised a company of volunteers, was commissioned a lieutenant in Colonel Dodges' regiment, and took part in the capture of Fort Erie where he was wounded.

In 1816, Judge Benjamin Wright appointed Canvass White as his assistant. In 1817, DeWitt Clinton sent White to England to study the English Canal System. Material which he gathered on that trip was used to solve many of the problems which arose later on the Erie.

Probably the greatest need in the construction of the Erie was a hydraulic cement which would harden under water. Such a cement could be purchased from England but the cost was so great that the Legislature refused to approve the purchase. One day when Canvass White was in Chittenango, he was approached by two young men whose names history did not record. They suggested to White that there was lime rock near the route of the Canal which might be what White was looking for. White took a sample, burned it, put it in a mortar and pulverized it with a pestle. After mixing it with sand, he made it into a ball and left it overnight. The next morning he found a ball of stone "hard as a miser's heart." The needed cement had been found. He obtained a patent for it, but permitted its use under the promise of the Canal Commission for a just compensation. However, the commissioners never received the necessary authority from the legislature for such compensation.

In 1825, Canvass' younger brother Hugh started a business in Chittenango manufacturing White's Water Proof Cement. Later he manufactured the cement in Roundout in Ulster County and later at the Rosendale Cement Works which produced most of the cement used on the Croton Aqueduct.

For several months in 1820, Canvass White was in charge of a party involved in leveling over and surveying different routes for the canal line; later that year he, with Benjamin Wright, worked east of Utica from Little Falls to the Hudson. In the spring of 1832, he was to lay out the Glens Falls feeder. Also in that year he panned and directed the building of the lock and dam between Troy and Waterford. Judge Wright had only praise for Canvass White, feeling that he could get sound advice from this young man on any engineering problem.

White later worked on a number of other projects, one of which was with Nathan Roberts on the main line canal in Pennsylvania; however, he is best known for his building of the Croton Waterworks which provided pure water for New York City. Later he worked on improving navigation of the Connecticut River and in 1827 was made chief engineer of the Delaware and Raritan Canal.

It was not surprising that, in 1834, his health broke down. He went to St. Augustine, Florida to try to regain his strength but died there one month later. He was buried in Princeton, New Jersey where his family lived. His death was a great loss especially to the budding new field of engineering. Accolades came from all over the country. When the project of the Chesapeake and Ohio Canal was conceived and an engineer was needed, Henry Clay said, "Get Canvass White; no man more capable; and while your faith in his ability increases, your friendship will grow into affection."

White's death was a great loss to Nathan Roberts who depended heavily on this bright young cousin who visited Roberts' home often and whose brilliant ideas were an inspiration.

The first section of the Erie Canal to be dug was set to start at Rome and to proceed eastward to Utica. Then different crews were to proceed at the same time eastward and westward until the Canal was finished. To many, the plan seemed foolhardy, since to the west, there was an almost impenetrable wilderness. Supplies would be difficult to obtain and to deliver to the canal route because of the absence of roads and of people to supply food; however, there were sound reasons for the decision to begin the canal in the middle of the state. First, the route from Rome to Utica was practically level so that no locks were needed and digging would be relatively easy and progress fast. This was important, because many people still considered the building of the Canal a foolish dream and fast results were needed to gain their support. Also, had the Canal started in Albany, the people in the West would have refused their support for a Canal which would never reach them. Conversely, had the Canal been started in the West, New Yorkers would have vetoed the whole project.

On the 4th of July, 1817, at dawn, a large number of citizens, the acting commissioner and engineers were present in Rome for the ground breaking ceremony to begin the Erie Canal. The Honorable Joshua Hathaway, one of the pioneers of the West, made a few pertinent observations on behalf of the citizens and then gave the spade to the commissioner who turned it over to Judge Richardson, the first contractor engaged in the work. There followed a speech by Colonel Young:

> "Fellow Citizens: We have assembled to commence the excavation of the Erie Canal. The work when accomplished will connect our western inland seas with the Atlantic Ocean. It will diffuse the benefits of internal navigation over a surface of vast extent, blessed with a salubrious climate and luxuriant soil, embracing a tract of country capable of sustaining more human beings than were ever accommodated by any work of the kind.

By this great highway, unborn millions will easily transport their surplus productions to the shores of the Atlantic, procure their supplies and hold a useful and profitable intercourse with all the maritime nations of the earth. The expense and labor of this great undertaking bears no proportion to its utility. Nature has kindly afforded every facility; we have all the moral and physical means within our reach and control. Let us proceed to the work, animated by the prospect of its speedy accomplishment and cheered with the anticipated benedictions of a grateful posterity."

Judge Richardson then thrust the spade into the earth and was followed by various citizens and laborers anxious to participate.

Roberts stood with bowed head as the benediction was pronounced. He was thrilled to be part of DeWitt Clinton's dream canal but uncertain of his ability. Imagine a canal three hundred thirty six miles long, forty feet wide at the surface and twenty eight feet at the bottom with a ten foot towpath. This canal must somehow overcome the fact that Lake Erie was five hundred sixty eight feet higher than the Hudson. The Canal must cross over valleys, rivers, creeks and must go through marshes and miles of solid stone. All this was to be in charge of two amateurs, Benjamin Wright and James Geddes whose only experience had been a bit of surveying. All of these misgivings passed through Roberts' mind during the ceremony; however, in spite of his doubts and those of many others, the Canal was begun.

On July 28, 1817, a son, DeWitt Clinton Roberts, was born to Lavinia and Nathan. The choice of the name is indicative of the high esteem in which Roberts held DeWitt Clinton. During the winter, Roberts again taught school at Whitesboro. He and Lavinia were forced to live in one room as the main farmhouse had been rented. As soon as spring came, Roberts returned to Rome and to his job as assistant engineer. In the fall, Lavinia and baby moved to the farm in Lenox.

In Roberts' crew, there was a young man, John B. Jervis, destined to become a famous engineer; however, at this time he was only beginning. Son of a carpenter, Jervis yearned for better than his common school education, but it was necessary for him to stay home to help support the family. It was the practice in the building of the Canal to let out contracts for short sections to local contractors. John's father was interested in bidding for one of these contracts and thought his son might gain useful information if he had a job on the Canal. John applied and was accepted, but because of lack of education and experience, he had to start at the bottom as an axeman. The axeman's job was the toughest, as he was to hack out the line in the swampy forests. Above him in rank were the target men or rodmen, next the chainmen (front and rear) above whom was the instrument man. In charge of all was Roberts, the party chief. As described by Jervis, "Our main ambition was to satisfy the chief of the party, N.S. Roberts, Esq., who was a man of austere manner who did not hesitate to speak plainly."

Jervis watched fascinated as the target men manipulated the instruments. After a while, he got up courage to ask some questions and to examine the instruments. The party generally regarded Roberts with a reverence which did not allow familiarity so that, for a time, Jervis did not approach him, but Roberts seemed to unbend and expressed his pleasure at the work of the axeman stating that he had never had a pair of axemen so skillful and efficient. He added that he was partial to men not afraid to work. On the last day of the season while the party was huddled in the swamp eating dinner, Jervis mustered up his courage and partly in joke and partly in earnest asked Roberts, "What will you give me to go with you next summer and carry one of those targets?" Roberts promptly replied, "Twelve dollars a month." Jervis promptly accepted.

Later he wondered if he could ever go beyond this with only a slight education. "The mystery of the level, the taking of sights, its adjustments and the computations of the observations" were all a mystery to him. He even thought Roberts might be joking, so he consulted his old friend Benjamin Wright who reassured him. Jervis began now seriously to prepare himself. At the recommendation of Roberts, Jervis bought two books on surveying which he studied diligently at night and when the weather did not allow work. One of these, *The Edinburgh Encyclopedia*, gave information on the mechanical studies of canals, water works, bridge centers and trusses. When he ran into difficult problems, Roberts, his mentor, was there to help.

On April 10, 1818, Jervis proudly, with target on shoulder, in the company of a dozen men, left for Geddesburg (later Syracuse). Except for Roberts, the party walked accompanied by a baggage wagon carrying necessary supplies. Because of muddy roads, only seven miles was made on the first day. It was the afternoon of the third day when Syracuse was reached. The problems for the party had hardly begun. In Syracuse, the party was organized for the work of locating the canal from Syracuse to Montezuma on the Seneca River, a distance of thirty-six miles. A few days later, there came a severe snowstorm which left six inches of snow on the ground. It was followed by a serve windstorm which shredded tents and destroyed supplies.

That spring, with the return of warm weather came the return of the mosquitoes. Mosquitoes proved to be one of the greatest dangers in the building of the Erie. Not only did they pester the men day and night, but they carried the dread malaria. One summer, work had to be completely halted, because so many men died of malaria that it was impossible to get men to take their places.

Another problem which harassed Roberts was jealousy among the men as to their positions. Occasionally, it was necessary for him to ask young aspirants of the profession of engineering to cut pegs and stakes and to clear the line. They considered these chores beneath their dignity and so, resentful, they worked slowly and slovenly. Young Jervis, however, endeared himself to Roberts because of his willingness to do any chore. As a result, although Roberts was the only one in the party deemed competent to compute the levels, he did allow Jervis to practice with the level. The same was true of map making. In this way, Jervis learned the skills which would make him one of America's great engineers. He commented later that all he knew, he had learned from Nathan Roberts.

There is no doubt that some of the men resented Roberts, for he was a perfectionist. He was critical of the target men if they made an error. He tried to impress upon them the importance of establishing a correct level. He was a hard taskmaster but was as hard on himself as on his men. With them, he walked the five miles from camp to work each day but with a half hour respite for lunch.

The location of the Canal was completed to the east bank of the Seneca River by the tenth of July—three months from the day the party left Rome, a distance of eighty miles by foot. The party returned to Rome where Jervis was put under David Bates, resident engineer of a division extending from Canastota in Madison County to Limestone Creek in Onondaga County, a distance of seventeen miles. Bates knew little about the use of leveling instruments, so he let Jervis use the instruments freely while he readily admitted that he could learn from Jervis.

At this point, Jervis and Roberts were separated. In 1820, Jervis was made a member of the Erie Canal's Engineering staff. Although the two men worked on different projects, they always held each other in the highest esteem and called on each other frequently for consultation.

4

DIFFICULTIES IN DIGGING THE CANAL

Due to a difference of opinion on the location through Rome, it was autumn, 1817, before the actual digging was started. First a sixty foot path was cleared with stakes placed forty feet apart. Then came the axemen, followed by the crews with shovels. The huge swamp to the south of Rome proved an enormous obstacle; however, finding workers was no problem. Men came from miles away to make "big" money. Hiring was done by small contractors who agreed to dig a certain section for an agreed price. It was up to them to hire the workers, to build a shack for housing twenty-four to forty men, to supply them with horses, shovels and scrapers, to feed them and to provide them with a daily ration of whiskey. With the need for speed, more than native workers were needed. Irish immigrants, many recruited from New York city by Canvass White, were lured by the promise of roast beef twice a day, whiskey and eighty cents a day wages, three times the amount paid for unskilled labor in Europe. Before the completion of the Canal, the Irish made up one fourth of the labor force.

The fourteen hour working day was unbelievably difficult as the route of the Canal went through marshes, virgin timberland, almost impenetrable underbrush, and muck. There was, however, no shortage of food in the Rome area. The wake up horn sounded a half hour before sunrise and called the men to breakfast—fried eggs, steak, sausage or pork chops, potatoes, cornbread, rolls, pancakes with molasses and syrup, fried mush with milk, tea, coffee, and buttermilk. The kitchen crew packed hearty lunches to be consumed during the lunch break. They came back in just before sundown for a big supper. Venison, bear, squirrel and partridges were plentiful along the Canal route, but the workers demanded beef, pork, and mutton. The men's appetites seemed insatiable and their capacity for work was boundless. Even after a week of working fourteen hours a day, they still had the energy to get roaring drunk on Saturday nights. Fights and brawls frequently ensued resulting in men showing up for work on Monday morning bearing the scars of battle-cuts, bruises and swollen hands. Roberts would frequently hear them from his tavern room as he worked on his maps and surveys. This was a lonely time for him, for in no way could he bring himself to associate with the brawling men. Whenever possible, he made short trips home to see his wife and small son. The people of Rome were anxious to see the completion of the digging of the Canal to the south or Rome, and with it, the departure of the wild Irish bog trotters.

Before they left, however, there was the Great Cedar Swamp to be conquered. For miles to the south of Rome, was an enormous swamp. The men found digging in this area almost impossible. At times, they were mired to their waists in mud; the muck literally pulled off their clothes. The men solved the problem by simply taking off all clothes with the exception of their shirts and slouch hats, protection against the mosquitoes. It was a sight to see them file back from work with the lower parts of their bodies covered only with black mud.

Progress on the canal was enhanced by American ingenuity in inventions to overcome problems. It has been said that necessity is the mother of invention and so it was on the Canal. Grubbing out the underbrush was extremely slow and tedious until someone attached cutting blades to a cast iron plow which cut through the shrubs and bushes in half the time. The tight construction schedule could not be met until a way was found to remove the tall trees in the path of the Canal. The machine which was devised consisted of an endless screw connected with a roller, cable, and crank. The cable was secured to a treetop and to the roller. As the crank was turned, the cable wound itself around the roller until the pressure toppled the tree. This still left the stump to be removed which was a more intricate problem. The machine invented for this job was a giant drum or cylinder mounted on wheels sixteen feet in diameter, with an axle twenty inches in diameter and thirty feet long. At the middle of the axle was attached a drum fourteen feet in diameter. A cable joined the stump to the drum. A team of horses or oxen was hitched to a rope which encircled the central drum. As the drum turned, the cable was drawn in and the stump was pulled from the ground. An operator of the stump puller with seven workers and four horses could extract forty large stumps in a day.

Even the traditional wheelbarrow was redesigned to meet the needs of the Canal. Jeremiah Brainard of Rome invented a new type of wheelbarrow with bottom an d sides made of a single board bent to semicircular shape. It was light and much easier to unload than the traditional model.

By late 1818, work on the Canal had progressed to the edge of the

Montezuma swampland. Montezuma, also called the Cayuga Marshes, a place avoided by both Indians and whites in pioneer days, is today a wildlife preserve but still a desolate place. When Roberts and his men were laying the line for the Canal, the swamp was so saturated that the men often worked in water to their chests. Canvass White described it as neither land nor water but "a streaky and unpleasant mixture of both." Impenetrable thickets of rushes barred their way with uncertain footing provided by the black mud. In Robert's words,

> "The most unhealthy part of the whole Canal was from Jordan in the Town of Camillus to Clyde Village in the Town of Golen, being very low or near the lowlands bordering the Seneca River and across the Cayuga Marshes which are six miles over as the Canal runs."

Irish workers kept their sense of humor as they tackled the swamp. Their song went as follows:

> "We are digging our ditch through the mire.
> Through the mud and slime and the mire, by heck!
> In our pants, up our sleeves, down our necks, by heck!
> The mud is our principal hire."

The men would dig and the next morning the ditch would be filled with mud. Retaining walls of planks had to be constructed. These had to be held in place by stakes driven through the muck to the clay beneath. The men's legs swelled from working in water, and leeches fastened onto them. Much worse, however, were the swarms of mosquitoes which attacked the men, leaving their eyes shut and hands so swollen that they were unable to hold tools. Smudge pots, called Montezuma necklaces, containing fire covered with green leaves producing a dense smoke were worn around the necks of the men. Perhaps they were effective in driving away the mosquitoes. Certainly they were effective in almost choking the men to death. Indians in the area had predicted death to the white men who entered the swamp in the summer, and they were proved right. With the coming of the malaria carrying anopheles mosquito, men began to die. During the digging in the swamp in the summer of 1819, men died by the hundreds—so many that work had to be discontinued until cold weather. No workers were available.

Treatment for the malarial chills and fever were bleeding, feverwort, snakeroot, green pigweed and Seneca oil (petroleum). A new drug from Peru called "Jesuits' bark" seemed to help. The bark contained quinine.

The unsung heroes who gave their lives to the Montezuma Swamp were buried in meadows along the way with little ceremony and with no stones to mark their resting places.

Cold weather seemed to be the greatest aid to overcoming the problem of the swamp. The mosquitoes were killed by the cold and it was found that the half frozen earth was easier to work than had been the muck of the summer.

5

PROGRESS

After two and a half years of work on the Erie, the Canal Commission decided to open the completed section of the Canal from Rome to Utica. It was a wise decision both politically and psychologically. This event tended to quiet the canal skeptics and increased tremendously the enthusiasm of those both east and west who anticipated the opening of the sections serving their areas.

On October 23, 1819, the first of many celebrations to come took place as the "Chief Engineer of Rome," named for Benjamin Wright and carrying Governor DeWitt Clinton, members of the Canal Commission, engineers and fifty notables towed by a single horse began its trip. Roberts, on hearing the news was thrilled at the practical manifestation of DeWitt Clinton's dream; however, he was involved with problems he knew he must face on the western section to which he had been assigned as chief engineer.

On December 6th, Roberts left for Canastota to see his family whom he had not visited for three months. Hardly had he arrived when, at midnight, Lavinia presented him with a baby daughter whom they named Mary Jane. Nathan felt that he could only stay home for a week and even during that week, he worked on plans for locks between Rochester and Clyde at Galen. Before his trip home, he had put the twenty mile section eastward from Rochester under contract to Holly and Seymour. At all times he felt the urgency for speed in the completion of the Canal.

Lavinia's life was a busy but lonely one at home with her two babies. The large house being built was not yet ready for occupancy. This was the only residence on the north side of the turnpike between Wampsville and Quality Hill. On the south side one half mile west of Roberts' was the home of Edom Bruce built by his father, General Joseph Bruce. The Roberts' farm was for the most part rented out on shares.

About the first of March, Roberts was back at work in the Perringian Swamp. The Canal was to be located down the Clyde River and through the Cayuga Marshes where quicksand became a problem. In April 1820, works was hampered when the work force at Palmyra was struck with fever and ague. Roberts found the area of Jordon in the Town of Camillus to the Village of Clyde most trying because of the marshes.

Judge Bates was put in charge of the building of the aqueduct at Rochester and of the Canal twenty miles east and west of Rochester. Early in 1820, another large celebration took place as the Erie was opened to navigation from Utica to Rochester. The packetboat "Lion of the West" left Rochester early on the morning of April 21st and proceeded to Lyons that afternoon with only one change of horses. It arrived in Syracuse the following day and continued on to Utica. Its average speed was five miles an hour. This speed created a wash which eroded the Canal banks, so a speed limit of four miles an hour was established with penalties for exceeding the limit.

On the 4th of July, 1820 there was a great celebration in Syracuse in which seventy-three boats took part. DeWitt Clinton was present at the grand affair and foolishly promised that the entire canal would be finished by 1823. In predicting this, he took note of the fact that two of the most difficult problems, the escarpment at Lockport and the Mohawk Falls, had not been approached, much less solved. His political enemies in Albany took note. He was running for reelection as governor but was so involved with the Canal that he had little time for campaigning. It was a narrow victory of only a few thousand votes, the tide swayed by the upstate voters.

The Legislature voted to borrow a million dollars in 1821 and another million in 1822 for canal construction. With a force of three thousand five hundred workers, the section between Utica and Little Falls was quickly completed, followed shortly by an extension to Schenectady.

By the end of the 1821 season, the Erie Canal had been opened for a distance of two hundred twenty miles. Traffic for the season was estimated at fourteen hundred boats carrying flour, salt, meat and farm products from Rochester to Schenectady where lines of passengers awaited transportation for the return trip. Although this was a fantastic accomplishment in little over four years, serious doubts began to be expressed that Clinton could make good his promise of completing the Canal by 1823. There still remained almost one hundred and fifty miles to be completed plus the aqueduct at Cohoes, the Schoharie Dam and the greatest challenge of all—Lockport.

DeWitt Clinton knew he had erred so, before his political enemies could accuse him, he admitted his error and extended the completion date to 1825. The opposition pounced on this gleefully saying that already six million had been spent and that Clinton would be back in 1825 with a still incomplete canal and asking for more money.

On October, 1823, a grand celebration was held as boats from the north (the Hudson river and Lake Champlain), joined those from the Erie in the still unfinished basin at Albany. The difficult stretch from Schenectady with its twenty-seven locks had been completed.

When in January 1824, the Legislature met, there was a request for an appropriation of another million dollars for the Canal. Clinton's enemies viciously attacked him for wasting money on the Canal and for using money to inflate his own ego by celebrations and publicity. With the public solidly behind him, Clinton dared them to remove him from office. The legislature voted the appropriations but removed Clinton from the board of the canal commissioners. Only a group of jealous, vengeful legislators could perpetuate such a stupid act on a man who had given seven years to a project almost completed.

At this time even with the Canal incomplete, prosperity had come to the areas served by the Canal. In 1824, three hundred thousand dollars in tolls were collected. Thirty-five hundred new buildings had been erected in Albany which had a population of sixteen thousand and wholesale business had quadrupled in two years.

Robersts did not attend the above mentioned celebrations. His entire concentration was westward where the work progressed steadily. The only problem was difficulty in getting stone and supplies to the canal site through a wilderness of trails. Each mile westward put Roberts a mile farther from the home and family he loved and made it more difficult for him to visit. He was extremely conscientious and so did not feel comfortable in leaving the work unsupervised. Roberts was frequently lonely as he was a quiet person who found it difficult to fraternize with the rough, uneducated workers who found relief in drinking, coarse talk and jokes at each others' expense. Upon occasion, he would have visitors, men like himself whose horizons and interests matched his own. In May 1821, such a group paid him a visit. Judge Wright, Judge Bates, engineers Myron Holley and William Bouck, and the Canal Commissioners came. They took Roberts on a trip to Niagara Falls where they visited all accessible parts on the American side and Goats' Island which divides the Falls. Here they noted the sixty acres of fertile soil, the dates 1769-1772 carved on trees by General Augustus Porter and his men. Roberts and his friends crossed the bridge built to the American side by Porter, forty feet over the torrent.

The party returned to the wilderness area which eventually became Lockport, where they once again stared in wonder at the sixty-foot-high, solid rock escarpment which presented the greatest obstacle to the canal builders. It stood directly in the path of the Canal. It could not be circumvented nor could the Canal be completed until the problem was overcome if the Canal was to end in the Buffalo/Lake Erie area.

Obviously a single lock was an impossibility. A system of combined locks must be devised, and the creativity and ingenuity of the entire corps of engineers were called into play.

"On a certain day, plans, specifications and estimates were to be presented to the Canal Board by all engineers employed by the State. Without consulting anyone and with but little aid from published works on the subject of engineering, he (Roberts) proceeded to draft his plan for the proposed structure. It consisted of five double-combined locks, of twelve feet each, working side by side. He had the satisfaction of being able to lay before the Canal Board his plan, complete in all its details of construction and of having it (over many others) unanimously adopted, and himself appointed to superintend its construction."

Roberts later described this as the greatest moment of his life.

In June, 1822, he left the remaining work in the Cayuga and Clyde marshes to Hiram Tibbets. From that date until the Canal was finished in 1825, Roberts was involved in work from Lockport to Buffalo.

6

LOCKPORT

Clinton's dismissal from the Canal Board had no measurable affect on the progress of the Canal. His good friend, Myron Holly, was put in charge, and the two worked together as they had all along. Roberts started his work at Lockport with the sound support of Clinton, a man whom he admired greatly.

Lockport was a dark, forbidding area covered with forests of hardwood trees of oak and black walnut. The only inhabitants were rattlesnakes so dangerous that even Indians detoured around the area. It did not, however, remain a desolate place for long after Roberts and his labor force arrived. This force numbered from three thousand to five thousand men. At first they were housed in tents, but as the enormity of the project became obvious, many decided to build permanent homes. So from a snake infested area arose the prosperous city of Lockport. In order to erect any kind of dwelling, great numbers of trees had to be cut down. Many homes were built over the remaining stumps, which served as tables and chairs within. Outside, a traveler had to weave his way down the main lane to avoid them. The city was called Stump City for many years.

The most difficult section of the Canal at Lockport was a three mile stretch southwest of the locks. The average rock cut was from twenty-five to thirty feet in depth. A problem immediately arose from the need for adequate drills. Appeals were sent out to New York and Philadelphia with no satisfactory response. Once more, American ingenuity came forth. A blacksmith in the area, named Botsford, fashioned a highly tempered drill which would produce the needed holes. After each hole was drilled, the DuPont blasting powder was placed inside, followed by a piece of brown paper. The warning "Look Out" was sounded, the paper was lit and the worker literally ran for his life. In a number of cases, he didn't run fast enough and was blown to bits.

The problem was that there was no exact formula for the depth of the hole or for the amount of powder to be inserted. After the explosion, rocks, some as heavy as twenty pounds, rained down on the town. Residents, even children, learned quickly to scurry for shelter when the warning was sounded. For two years residents of Lockport were bombarded by the sounds of constant explosions.

One problem which resulted from the blasting was the accumulation of rubble below in the canal bed. The route for the workers with wheelbarrows was uphill, and they soon found that the mountain of stone was growing much faster than it could be removed. Once more, American inventiveness was resourceful. Orange Dibble who lived in the area solved the problem with a horse operated crane which would be placed above a cut. A wooden bucket was lowered to the cut below, filled with blasted stone, and raised to the bank above. These cranes were placed approximately seventy feet apart along the route of the construction. The debris was piled along the route of the Canal producing an unsightly wall seventy feet in height at places. The canal builders, intent on meeting Clinton's deadline, did not worry over disposition of the debris, and for years to come, the residents of Lockport labored cleaning up the stone.

7

THE ROBERTS' HOME

During the years that Nathan Roberts spent at Lockport, he was approximately one hundred and seventy-five miles from home, so that a trip home was of necessity a rare occurrence; however, on March eleventh he started on a long deferred trip to Canastota. The cost of the trip is of interest:

Lockport to Ridge Road	$ .50
Ridge Road to Rochester	2.50
Rochester to Canandaigua	1.00
Canandaigua to Lenox	3.25
	$7.50

At the Canal basin, Roberts obtained a horse. As he rode through the village, he was once again amazed at the growth of the village since his last visit. He spent little time, however, visiting with the villagers whom he saw, for the was anxious to get home. His one stop was at his mill on Canastota Creek where he found all in good working order. From the mill, he could see the tall chimneys of his home. When he had last been there, there were still a few finishing details to be added to the house. It had taken three years to build it, and he was anxious to see the finished job.

Roberts had bought the land making up the home farm in 1813. The fifty acres was bounded on the east by the present Peterboro Street, on the west by Stroud Street, on the north by James Street, and on the south by the Seneca Turnpike. In addition, Roberts later bought six hundred acres across the turnpike from the home farm.

It was not until 1820 that he decided to build his home on this land and this became his home farm. Previous to this, the land, having been cleared, had been mainly a sheep farm with a small number of cattle and pigs cared for by a local manager. At one time, there were as many as eight hundred and fifty sheep on the farm. Even after the home was built and the family moved in, the farm was primarily a sheep farm.

Roberts wisely located his house approximately two hundred fifty feet from the center of the turnpike so that even with the widening of the road, there remained a large front lawn giving a proper setting for the house. The house, a large white clapboard of Georgian design had a two story center section flanked by two perfectly matched one story wings. On the front of each wing, there was a porch which brought the wings in line with the main section. On the main section, there were pilasters flush with the house giving the effect of pillars without the sometimes cumbersome effect of the traditional Greek revival. There were three front doors, one for each wing, and the main door with an arched fanlight and glass side panels of leaded glass on which were superimposed circular flower designs.

Attached to the rear of the house, there were four arched sleigh sheds under which the horses found protection and oats while the owners visited inside. Attached to the sleigh shed was the carriage house with an upper story which served as quarters for the coachman. Three enormous chimneys topped the house to serve the seven fireplaces within. Outside there was the traditional red barn with a shingled roof and the smokehouse of red Flemish brick with white trim.

The house was completed in the 1820s for $2,500. In the 1950's it was completely restored to its original state.

As you enter the house, there is a large hall which contained the stairway with its long stair rail of walnut. In the hall as well as in the library and living room, there are hand carved lilies at each window and door frame. The floors throughout most of the house are of pine matched boards approximately five to nine inches wide. The hand carving over the fireplace in the library is unique. It is the Hessian sunburst design and is said to have been carved by a Hessian soldier who fell in love with America after the War of 1812, settled on Quality Hill and there practiced his trade.

The most formal and certainly the most beautiful room in the house is the living room which features an ornate frieze of grape clusters supported by carved wood between the side walls and the ceiling. The fireplace is of Italian veined marble, possibly installed about 1896.

The dining room features a huge fireplace complete with swinging crane and beehive baking oven. The hearth is made of fossilized sandstone. The fireplace is flanked by two doors, one opening into a large closet for dishes, the other to a stairway leading to an upstairs bedroom. White wainscoting made of two boards each thirteen inches wide, placed horizontally and topped by a chair rail surround the room. Other features of the room are plate rails and one curved wall.

The working kitchen was in the basement. The fireplace topped by a mantel of solid pine filled almost an entire wall and also featured a swinging crane and beehive oven. Next to the fireplace is an iron cauldron thirty inches in diameter and eighteen inches deep which provided the family with a constant supply of hot water. In front of the fireplace and cauldron was a huge hearth of Flemish brick. This room is now a recreation room.

Upstairs there are five bedrooms. The attic above goes the length of the house and is completely plastered. It was probably used for bedrooms for servants.

We do not know who the builders were but strongly suspect, because of the mathematical symmetry, that Nathan Roberts drew the plans himself. In 1938, the Architects Editorial Committee, after surveying old homes throughout the United States, chose this house to be included with a handful of other New York homes in *The Great Georgian Houses of America*. Blueprints of the house are on file in the National Archives in Washington, D.C.

An undated view of the Canal showing the towpath and mules.

A view of the Canal looking west from Canastota showing the towpath as well as a railroad bridge spanning the Canal so that coal could be dumped into the barges below.

Plans for the Nathan Roberts Flight of Locks at Lockport, circa 1825.

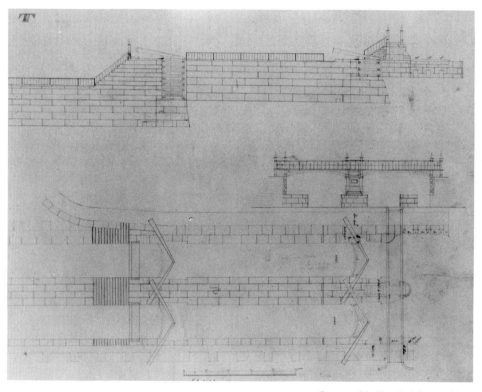

Another plan for the Flight of Locks at Lockport.

"Entrance to the Harbor, Lockport" from Colden's <u>Memoir</u>, (1825).

View shewing the progress of the work on the Loch Section

Detail of 1839 view of Lockport at the commencement of the first enlargement of the Erie Canal.

Lithograph of a lock at Lockport with a view of the Canal looking east.

8

Lafayette's Visit

In June 1825, construction at Lockport was still in progress when the Marquis de Lafayette came to visit. He had returned to America in August 1824 for a five thousand mile tour of America. He was welcomed everywhere as a hero of the Revolution. He arrived in Buffalo from a Lake Erie steamboat, visited the Falls, the Tuscarora Reservation and proceeded to Lockport where he was welcomed by Roberts. Lafayette was greeted by a tremendous blast of what sounded like artillery fire. The canal crew had planted gunpowder charges every few feet in the rock wall from the locks to the present site of Hitchen's Bridge and the resulting explosions sounded like hundreds of cannons fired at intervals seconds apart. Lafayette was extremely pleased. "The very rocks rend to welcome me" was his response. Later at a banquet in the Washington House, in speaking of the locks at Lockport and of Niagara Falls, he stated that "Lockport and the county of Niagara contain the greatest natural and artificial wonders, second only to the wonders of freedom and equal rights."

Lafayette's secretary gives us an excellent view of the village.

"I have nowhere seen the activity and industry of man brought into operation against natural difficulties as in this young village. The sound of axe and hammer are everywhere heard. On one side trees fall which are fashioned by the hands of carpenters on the same spot in the form of houses; on another, in a public square, which is only marked out, a large inn already opens its doors to the new citizens who have as yet no other shelter. There are hardly to be found in the village the means of satisfying the first wants of life; and yet besides a schoolhouse where the children can be instructed while their fathers are building houses to shelter them, is erected a press which issues a newspaper that informs the workmen during their hours of repose, how the magistrates of the people perform the task with which they have been honored.

In the streets marked out in the forest, and still embarrassed with the trunks of trees and thick branches, luxury already presents herself in light carriages drawn by fine horses, and finally in the midst of these encroachments of civilization on savage nature, that great canal is proceeding with a rapidity which seems to mark the hand of union, will at the same time diffuse life and abundance in the deserts through which it passes.

9

On To Buffalo

On June 24, 1825, Roberts stood at the top of the double locks at Lockport and surveyed his work of the past three years. Roberts was a handsome man of slightly bulky build. His blonde hair blew in the breeze and his blue eyes seemed bluer, accented by the deep tan acquired during his constant exposure to wind and sun. Today there was added sparkle in his eyes because the capstone was to be laid. The double locks stood as silent monuments to the diligence of this man. The challenge of Lockport had been met and conquered.

Later in the day, with Governor Clinton, Commissioner Holley, Benjamin Wright and Roberts in attendance as well as several lodges and the people of Lockport, the capstone at Lockport was laid with Masonic ceremony. The oration was given by Rev. Cumming of Rochester. This was Nathan Roberts' finest hour.

Roberts, however, was not one to rest on his accomplishments. The route from Lockport to Buffalo was not yet completed. Roberts was acutely aware of Clinton's promise to complete the canal in the year of 1825. The stimulus to the workers was provided by barrels of whiskey placed along the canal route. When the Irish crew reached a barrel, they could relax and enjoy.

With the men working diligently and under good supervision, Roberts left for a brief assignment to Niagara Falls on August 10th. He had been invited to study and to map a plan for by-passing the Falls. He worked there for ten days and made a final report. We do not know whether his plan or some other was adopted when the Welland Canal was built in 1833.

After this project and after a short stop at Lockport, Roberts returned to his home in Canastota. After his long absence, there was much to do on the farm. During the visit, he took Lavinia and the children on a trip to her old home in Whitesborough where they were welcomed by friends and family. There were now four Roberts children—DeWitt, aged 8, Mary Jane,6, Albert, 3, and Lavinia Catherine, a babe in arms. This seems to be the only time Lavinia and her family returned to visit the

Whites. Perhaps the reason was the wide political differences between Roberts and Hugh White. White was a staunch Whig and Republican. In 1844, he was chosen a representative to Congress where he served three terms.

Roberts left home again on September 6, to inspect and to speed up preparations for the final ceremony planned for October 24. The plan was that boats would begin the trip from Buffalo to Albany where they would be jointed by a flotilla from the Champlain Canal. All would continue on to the Atlantic at Sandy Hook. The wedding of the waters was about to begin. DeWitt Clinton's dream and his promise were to be fulfilled. There was now a canal which traversed all of New York State.

Excitement on the route of the Canal was at a fever pitch as each village along the way prepared for its own celebration. When the flotilla left Buffalo, word was went to New York City of the departure by a series of cannon fire, each village sending off its cannon when it heard the one before. In an amazing eight-five minutes, the word was received in New York city. Even villages passed in the night, welcomed the boats with cut-out billboards behind which lanterns were placed. Only in the village of Rome was there no celebration. Instead there was a funeral march accompanied by a dirge. Alas the canal had by-passed the village, a route having been chosen to the south instead.

Hundreds of accounts have been written describing the most impressive celebration New York City had ever had. One more was to be added —that of Nathan Roberts who was there. In his low key conservative writing, he described the event as follows:

> "The Governor, DeWitt Clinton and all the canal commissioners, the lieutenant governor and many heads of departments of state, a committee from the City of New York, from Albany, Buffalo, Utica, Rochester and other places attended at Lockport and an appropriation address was delivered at the head of the lake by Judge Birdsall. The whole was brightening and amending to the highest degree. The number of people present was very great. The boats from the lake pursued their course to the Hudson to make the long contemplated voyage across the country. I witnessed this first voyage and went to New York and to Sandy Hook. The whole was truly splendid. At distances of about eight or ten miles along the canal, a heavy piece of cannon was placed and the glad news was communicated from the lakes to the ocean and back to the lakes in about one hour and forty minutes, on the 24th of October, when the first boats started. As the boats passed these cannons, a salute of several guns was fired and at every village great numbers were col-

lected to join in the good feeling and to celebrate the completion of the grand canal.

From Albany the brilliancy of the scene was augmented by a fleet of steam boats 21 in number, who took the canal boats in tow. Every town we passed gave cheers and guns, raised flags, and in the night illuminated their homes. At West Point, soldiers fired, the officers came on board with their bands of music and at daylight the whole fleet ranged in front of the city and formed in line. Several foreign ships saluted our fleet, which was handsomely returned by our Commodore Rhyne, by sailing around them in the flag boat, the Chancellor Livingston.

About 10 o'clock the procession was formed in the city and the boats with great additions formed a line and sailed first up East River and took in the Commodore Chauncey, (with his fine marine band) and many other distinguished officers.

Several large ships were draped out in the flags of all nations and lay in tow, and the whole united to join the waters of the lakes to the waters of the ocean. At 2 o'clock the ceremony was performed by Governor Clinton on board the flag boat Chancellor Livingston, and during the performance the whole fleet formed a circle and heard a speech on the occasion from Dr. Mitchell. As our fleet entered the dominions of old Neptune, we were saluted by the United States schooner Granpas who lay at anchor off the Hook and fired minute guns as we sailed around her. At the close she manned her yards and cheered and was then taken in tow by a steamboat and the whole fleet returned in the same style to the city and landed at the battery about 3 o'clock, and formed the grand procession in the city, the main part of which was unseen. Everybody seemed to excel and it was said that not less than fifty thousand strangers were in the city. The day was fine and no accidents happened to mar the good feelings. The whole was finished by a grand display of fire works and the city illuminated and a splendid canal ball at the New Astor. To attempt to describe these scenes is all that can be done. No description can equal the reality."

Roberts remained in the city for a few days no doubt taking in the sights. If Lavinia Roberts thought that her husband would return home to farm after the triumph of the Erie, she was dreaming indeed. Knowledge of his accomplishment at Lockport was widespread, and it was thought that he could unravel any complicated canal problem. Even before the grand celebration, he had been contacted by John Randall and Judge Wright for consultation on the Chesapeake & Delaware Canal.

After a few days in New York City, Roberts left for that consultation.

10

THE SUCCESS OF THE ERIE

The success of the Erie Canal was truly phenomenal. In 1828, tolls on the Erie amounted to $765,000. It was not unusual to see fifty boats a day leaving Albany; thousands of people realized their dream of going west. Farmers in the west sent grain, timber and furs to eastern markets in return for manufactured goods. Cities grew like mushrooms. In describing the growth of Syracuse, Col. William Stone, editor and writer said, "Syracuse seemed to him like a city risen by enchantment where nine years before, when he had visited the site, there had been only some five or six scattered tenements . . . the whole being surrounded by a desolate, poverty-stricken country enough to make an owl weep to fly over it."

The growth of Rochester was even more phenomenal. A wilderness in 1812, ten years later it had a population of twenty-seven hundred and by 1828, eleven thousand. A description of Rochester in 1827 states:

"Everything in this bustling place seems to be in motion. The very streets seem to be starting up of their own accord, ready made and looking as fresh and new as if they had been turned out of a workman's hands but an hour before. The canal banks were at some places still unturfed, the lime seemed hardly dry in the masonry of the aqueduct, in the bridges and in the numberless great saw mills and manufactories. In many of these buildings, the people were at work below stairs, while at the top, the carpenters were busy nailing on the planks of the roof . . . I cannot say how many churches, court houses, jails and hotels I counted creeping upward. Here and there we saw great warehouses with out window sashes but half filled with goods and furnished with hoisting cranes, ready to pick up the huge pyramids of flour barrels, bales and boxes lying in the streets. I need not say that these half-finished, whole finished and embryo streets were crowded with people, carts, cattle, pigs far beyond the reach of numbers and as all these were lifting up their voices together, in keeping with the clatter of hammers, the ringing of axes and the creaking of machinery, there was a fine concert."

In addition to the growth of cities, the Erie was responsible for the birth of innumerable villages which sprang up to serve the farmers in the hinterlands.

Even before the Erie was completed, other states looked on with alarm and envy. Canal mania swept the country. Old projects were renewed and new navigation companies formed. Even in New York, towns not on the Canal began to clamor for feeders.

Boston considered and had made surveys for a canal joining Boston to Albany via Fitchburg and the Connecticut River. The obstacle was the Berkshires which necessitated a tunnel. The legislature turned down the project when an estimated cost of $6,023,172 was announced.

In 1821, Maine incorporated the Cumberland and Oxford from the Fore River to Segago Lake.

In 1822, an old project to unite Providence and Worcester along the Blackstone River was revived.

In 1823, the Chesapeake and Delaware, after being bogged down for some time, got going again, and the Delaware and Hudson began excavation.

In 1825, a company was chartered to build a canal from the Illinois River to Lake Michigan. It never got started.

In 1825, Ohio planned an extensive canal system including two between Lake Erie and the Ohio River. The Chesapeake and Ohio connecting the Potomac River with the Ohio Valley was being considered.

New companies such as the Hampshire and Hamden to connect Northampton, Massachusetts to New Haven, Connecticut and the Delaware and Hudson to give an outlet for the Lackawanna anthracite coal were formed. The Morris Canal and Banking Company was formed to build another anthracite-carrying canal across the state of New Jersey from the Delaware River to the New York harbor.

The James River and Kanawha Canal was already under construction. Activities in the State of Pennsylvania were the most complicated of all and will be dealt with later in this account.

Some of the above mentioned attempts proved profitable. Many remained only dreams but none even approached the success of the Erie.

In addition to the economic wealth it brought New York, the Erie opened up a whole new world to the inhabitants. Banks were multiplying, insurance companies, steamboat, pike and canal companies, mills and factories provided new occupations for mill hands and operators, machinists, mechanics, engineers, clerks, bookkeepers, gate and lock tenders—on and on—there was work for all who had in the past had only the option of farming.

In an expansive statement about the forces responsible for the creation of the Erie DeWitt Clinton not only identified the types of individu-
als who played a part, but he also suggested the democratic process of
nation and state building which took place. In the first class of people
responsible for the Canal he placed the dreamers like George Washington
who saw the eventual joining of the vast western wilderness with the
Atlantic coast. In the second class he grouped those who saw the possibility of a canal from the Great Lakes to the Hudson and so to the harbor at
New York City. In the third group were those who, like himself, saw the
need in 1810 to take positive steps to bring about needed improvement s
in the existing navigation facilities operating in the corridor from Albany
along the Mohawk westward to Rome and beyond the Great Lakes. Finally, he grouped all of the legislators, commissioners, surveyors, engineers to be, contractors and laborers who completed the takes. In this last
very large group he also included both the public spirited citizens who
supported the project and the government officials such as the lieutenant
governor, the comptroller and the attorney general. Although this classifi-
cation was the work of a consummate politician it revealed the statesman-
like dreams of a great leader.

11

CHESAPEAKE AND DELAWARE

The obvious advantages of joining the Delaware and Chesapeake Bays had been apparent for many years. Even a child could see that a canal of twenty-one miles which could save five hundred miles by sea would be an advantage to all needing transportation of goods and people. The dreamers imagined a federal system of inland waterways in which the Chesapeake and Delaware would be followed by a canal cut across New Jersey between the Delaware and the Raritan. A continuous inland waterway would then be open from Hampton Roads to Narragansett Bay and the headwaters of the Hudson and the Mohawk. To the south, the Dismal Swamp Canal would extend its channel to Albermarle Sound and the bays and inlets of South Carolina. Such a grandiose scheme, however, did not take into consideration the selfish interests in the diffuse areas involved.

As early as 1764 and 1769, surveys for a waterway connecting the Chesapeake and Delaware Bays had been made; however, lack of money caused interest to dwindle. The Revolution, of course, brought to a halt any progress. It was not until 1802 with Maryland joining Pennsylvania and Delaware in chartering the Chesapeake and Delaware Canal Company that work began.

The public subscribed for $400,000 of its stock of which perhaps as much as forty percent was paid. Hopes ran high that the canal could be completed in two or three years. It was to be a short canal, approximately twenty miles from bay to bay. By making use of the navigable water of the two little rivers, Apoquimene and Bohemia, the miles of canal to be dug would be much less than that. However, at the end of the year, when it was revealed that $100,000 had been wasted on needless surveys and other preliminaries, the bottom fell out of the promotion and stockholders refused to pay the assessments. The company failed and the project was abandoned.

For the next ten years, the Chesapeake and Delaware lay moribund, seemingly without hope of ever being revived. Then in 1822, the State of Pennsylvania pumped life into it. Admittedly it was acting in its own self-interest, but it was the only source from which the push to restore confidence in building the canal could have come. Financially, Delaware was in no position to do it, nor was Maryland, meaning Baltimore, ready to open Chesapeake Bay trade to Philadelphia.

By presenting the project as an internal improvement affecting the prosperity of three states, Pennsylvania, the richest and politically most powerful of the former colonies, succeeded in winning the endorsement of the federal government and a commitment of $500,000. Pennsylvania contributed $100,000 and induced Maryland to underwrite an obligation of $50,000. Little Delaware followed with a modest $25,000. With confidence restored and interest aroused as never before, private investors swelled the total money committed to over one million dollars.

Dr. Benjamin Wright was appointed permanent engineer; however, because of his continuing work on the Erie, he was not immediately available. The second choice was John Randle (the name Randle is variously spelled Randall, Randel, and Randla). Randle had been previously employed as an assistant engineer by the original Chesapeake and Delaware Company and had been dismissed for insisting that the route being taken would not provide enough water to get the canal over the backbone of the peninsula, while a course farther south would. He shortened the length of the canal to thirteen miles but at a terrific price in men, money and time, his grit and determination being no substitute for the engineering skill he did not possess.

The backbone of the peninsula was solid granite for a distance of one and a half miles, from seventy-six to ninety feet deep and sixty feet wide. Randle did not realize the enormity of the task he had undertaken. Although, at times, there were twenty-five hundred men working, progress was infinitesimal. Tools were primitive, and there were frequent landslides, one of which dumped 375,000 cubic yards of dirt into the partly dug canal. Black powder was still the only available explosive and Randle was not experienced in its use. Scores of workers were killed or maimed.

It was at this point that Roberts was called in. His expertise at Lockport in the use of black powder was desperately needed. He carefully examined the project taking notes and making maps and diagrams. He found that three dams would be necessary to supply the canal with water, a fact that Randle had not realized. In practical application, Roberts instructed Randle in the amount and proper placement of the dangerous black powder for certain types of rock formations. Roberts was involved in this project for about six weeks. Although there is nor mention of it in Roberts' journal, it is logical to suppose that he visited his birthplace at Piles Grove, New Jersey while in this area. The distance from the northern/eastern canal entrance to Piles Grove was only about forty miles.

When his consultation was complete, Roberts returned to Canastota to his home and family. As he stepped from the canal boat, he was once again amazed at the rapid growth of the village which been non-existent eight years before. New shops of all kinds were being built along the Canal, and the canal basin was jammed with boats loading produce from the surrounding fertile farmland. Other boats unloaded goods of all sorts, and packet boats tooted impatiently. The Peterboro street road penetrated farther into the hinterland each time Roberts returned home. Roberts stopped in the store which Reuben Hawley had built on the canal bank and in which John and Daniel Crouse ran a profitable grocery store.

Many welcomed and congratulated him, but his stay in the village was brief, for he was anxious to get home. After obtaining a horse at the livery south of the canal basin, he rode along Peterboro Street road noting the harness manufacturing establishment of Aleazer Lewis, the brick plant, the A.D. Van Hoosen and Spencer businesses. He noted the location of the lot on the corner of Peterboro and Center Streets which John Crouse had bought and on which he would soon build the Crouse Block. Roberts cut diagonally across fields which in summer would be golden wheat to check his mill on the Canastota Creek. From the mill, he could see smoke rising from the home of Reuben Perkins. Still traveling in a diagonal direction on his own land, he reached the Seneca Turnpike slightly more than a quarter of a mile from the mill. From here he could see the tall chimneys of his home. To the south rose the gentle hills which Roberts had always admired, for he was a lover of nature. He spurred his horse on, for he was tired and he anticipated the joyous welcome he would receive from his family. He would also be welcomed by Catherine White, his wife's young sister who had lived with them since 1824. Roberts checked his pack containing Christmas gifts for them all. What a holiday it would be!

As usual, it was to be a short visit, because immediately after Christmas he had to return to Lockport where he closed out all business concerning the Erie with a Colonel Bank, Canal Commissioner.

On January 1, we find Roberts at Niagara Falls. The State of New York had employed him to make a survey of a route for a ship canal around the Falls. He worked for two weeks at the Falls and then returned home to polish up his report. At home, he worked in the library where he had had installed a floor to ceiling book closet to house his magnificent collection of over three hundred books. Roberts was a meticulous worker in whatever he did. His report bears witness to this (see appendix).

On February 1, he left for Albany where he stayed for a month. After turning in his report, he spent the remaining time visiting with friends and testing the political climate. This time combined with another ten days at home represented a much needed vacation, a luxury which he hardly ever allowed himself. Already he was looking forward to work on a dual appointment as engineer for the main line of the Pennsylvania Canal and as a consultant for the Chesapeake and Ohio Canal.

12

THE PENNSYLVANIA CANAL

Only belatedly did Pennsylvania realize the threat to her economic security from the north and from the south. To the north, DeWitt Clinton was building the Erie with unbelievable speed. This was expected to provide an income from which "the whole expense of this magnificent operation would be defrayed in a few years, and an immense revenue would be secured to the State. This would enable it to patronize literature and science, to promote education, morality and religion, to encourage agriculture, manufactures and commerce."

Philadelphia saw that her goods would have to go around by sloop or steamboat to Albany and then west by the canal. Thus she could not compete with New York, Albany, Rochester or Buffalo.

To the south lay the threat of Baltimore with its toll free National Road, and with talk of a canal up the Potomac and on to the Ohio.

In December 1823, the Pennsylvania Legislature appointed a commission to report on the feasibility of a canal from Philadelphia to Pittsburgh. On April 1, 1824, a board of three canal commissioners was named. Unfortunately, Pennsylvania was not lucky enough to have a "water level" route as did New York. In any canal attempt, the Allegheny Mountains stood as a barrier to the West; however, the Committee reported that such a canal was perfectly practical. "The route suggested led from Philadelphia to the Susquehanna near Harrisburg, thence followed the Susquehanna and Juniata to a point near Hollidaysburg on the slope of the main range of the Alleghenies; it then would pass through that ridge by a tunnel four miles long reaching the forks of the Little Conemaugh and Allegheny Rivers and on to Pittsburgh." Since many people had never seen or even heard of a tunnel, a definition was included. A tunnel was "a hole like a well dug horizontally through a hill or mountain." The cost of the canal from the Susquehanna to Pittsburgh was estimated at three million dollars (which probably would not have paid for the proposed tunnel). Great benefits would ensue. The tolls would support the government, educate every child in Pennsylvania and guarantee Philadelphia the title of metropolis of the United States.

All were not convinced, however. For a year, the argument waged between proponents and opponents of the canal. Opposed to the canal were tavern owners and turnpike collectors, railroad advocates, those inhabitants not living near the route of the canal and some few wise men who realized the expense which would be involved. The proponents, however, confidently pushed ahead, and a bill for the construction of a canal passed both houses in February 1826.

Whereas Pennsylvania lacked the geographic advantages of New York, it had at hand the engineering knowledge gained from nine years' work on the Erie. Immediately the names of Roberts and Geddes came to mind and the canal veterans were tapped for help on the Pennsylvania Canal.

On March 26, 1826, Roberts left for Philadelphia where he joined Geddes. Together they had decided that an all-water route was practically impossible and certainly too costly. Their plan was for work to begin simultaneously at the ends of the Canal. From the east, the Canal would go up the Juniata River form the Susquehanna to Hollidaysburg at the foot of the Alleghenies. in the west the canal would follow the Allegheny River as far as the Conemaugh and follow that stream to the base of the mountain barrier. Between the eastern and western sections, there was a gap to be traversed by means of a railroad made up of a series of inclined planes.

Work on the Pittsburgh section progressed at a rapid pace; however, on July 7, 1827, Roberts stopped his work on the Canal because of a cut in pay. He returned to Canastota.

He had been home for only two weeks when he was solicited to examine the water supply on the summit below the forks of the Chenango, Oriskany and Oneida creeks. The surveying took three weeks.

While Roberts was busy on this job, the canal commissioners in Pennsylvania were in emergency session. Panic had set in at the loss of their principal engineer. Hardly had Roberts returned home when he received a new appointment from Pennsylvania at the handsome salary of thirty-six hundred dollars a year plus all personal and traveling expenses.

The Pennsylvania Canal as it was built by Roberts and Geddes was unique although not entirely original. The inclined plane had been used at South Hadly Falls in Massachusetts. Benjamin Wright had used the same principle when he built the planes for the Delaware and Hudson Canal Company. James Renwick had installed a series of inclined planes on the Morris Canal. All of this was known to Roberts, Geddes and to

Canvass White who had been called in for consultation when construction of the Portage Railway, the name given to the section across the Allegheny Mountains, was contemplated. The three engineers decided on an innovation; instead of a series of connected planes, "They would build separate planes and by means of horse-drawn cars running on rails move freight and passengers from the head of one plane to the foot of the next." The length of the Portage Railway was approximately thirty-seven miles—ten and one tenth miles on the eastern slope and twenty-six and one half on the western. This link made it possible to travel from Philadelphia to Pittsburgh.

For one wishing to make the trip, it was not easy. First, the traveler gave his name and address to an agent of the transport company the day before the trip. He was picked up the next morning with his luggage. At the railroad station, he boarded one of two small cars coupled together with the luggage on the roof and pulled by two horses. Just outside of Philadelphia the cars rolled onto the first inclined plane, twenty-eight hundred feet in length with a rise of one hundred eighty-seven feet. The cars were pulled up the grade by a huge hawser connected to a stationary steam engine. The horses were hooked on again at the summit and travel was resumed at the rate of nine to ten miles an hour. At Lancaster the passengers spent the night. At 4:00 a.m. they were awakened to continue their journey to Columbia where the railroad ended and the Canal began.

At 4:00 p.m. each week day, a horn announced that a packet was ready to go. The Canal went along the southern bank of the Susquehanna through Middletown and Harrisburg to a point opposite the junction of the Susquehanna and the Juniata. Here a dam formed a pool across which a bridge two thousand two hundred thirty-one feet long with a two story towpath had been built. On the west bank at the junction, the Canal forked with the Susquehanna division to the right. The main line crossed the Juniata by an aqueduct seven hundred feet long and continued westward.

One hundred and seventy-two miles from Columbia, the Canal reached Hollidaysburg where the Canal ended and the Portage Railroad began. Here the passengers spent the third night out. The trip over the mountain started at 5:00 a.m. in cars carrying a hundred passengers, each following closely one on another. It was three and three quarters miles to the foot of the first incline. The inclined planes were operated by stationary engines—one car ascending as another descended. The horses were hitched on and pulled the car for two miles. Then came another incline and so on for five inclines and five levels. The summit was reached by 8:00 a.m. and the passengers had a treat of breakfast at one of two lovely inns with a beautiful view as a bonus.

On a western slope, there were also five winches and five levels; however, the levels were each longer, one being thirteen and a half miles long.

The levels had grades of from 14 to 20 feet to the mile. At the Staple Bend of the Conemaugh, four miles east of Johnstown, there was a tunnel 901 feet long, the third in America and the longest. At Johnstown, the Canal began again and continued along the banks of the Conemaugh, Kiskiminetas and the Allegheny Rivers to Pittsburgh, a distance of 104 miles.

The Canal trip may sound slow, long and exhausting, but the alternatives were much worse. To go west at the time, one could go on horseback which was a much slower trip and on which the rider could carry few of his possessions. He was exposed to all kinds of weather and frequently he had to break his own trails. The few roads were no more than trails. Some hardy souls attempted the trip in Conestoga wagons only to tell tales of broken wheels, washed out roads and weeks of misery. Farmers in the west who sent their produce east in wagons found that it did not pay. The hazardous trip, the possibility of loss of crops and the high cost discouraged them, forcing more and more to turn to the rivers leading to New Orleans.

The Pennsylvania Canal never approximated the success of the Erie for a number of reasons. The Erie had a head start on the Pennsylvania as it had been finished sooner. The cost of the Pennsylvania Canal was far greater than that of the Erie. A large part of the cost was in the attempt to meet many demands of Pennsylvania citizens for innumerable subsidiary canals. At one point, the State of Pennsylvania was almost bankrupted by these demands.

The great obstacle on the Erie, the Lockport escarpment, could be surmounted in a few hours. To cross the Allegheny mountain in Pennsylvania was a matter of two days thus making for a much longer journey and for a more expensive one, on the Pennsylvania Canal.

Another factor which reduced profits on the Pennsylvania Canal was competition from the Cumberland Road. This road ran west from Cumberland, Maryland, and reached the Ohio River at Wheeling, Virginia (now West Virginia)! It was finished in 1817.

In spite of all the above factors, the Pennsylvania Canal must be deemed a success. It moved thousands of people to the west and tons of cargo east. The passengers were more comfortable and the goods moved cheaper and safer than transportation offered by horse or wagon. It must be considered a vital factor in the westward movement.

At the same time that Nathan Roberts received his second appointment as chief engineer on the Pennsylvania Canal, he had received an appointment from the Secretary of War, General Charles Fenton Moore, to be a member of the board of Engineers of the Chesapeake and Ohio Canal Company at a salary of $3000 a year. Starting in December 1828 and for the next two years, he worked on various aspects of this canal. Until August 1829, Roberts worked on and completed the revision and location of the Canal from Cumberland to Pittsburgh.

13

The Chesapeake and Ohio

Even before the Revolution, George Washington obtained passage of a bill empowering those who would engage in the work to open the Potomac from the Tidewater to Will's Creek. He also included improvements to the James River. His plans were interrupted by the War, but soon after, he approached Jefferson on the possibility of internal improvements. Washington suggested the appointment of commissioners to examine the James and Potomac Rivers to search out the best portages and streams running into the Ohio and on to the Great Lakes. As he said, "The western settlers stand as it were, upon a pivot. The touch of a feather would turn them either way. Until the Spaniards threw difficulties their way, they looked down the Mississippi—and they looked that way for no other reason than because they could glide gently down the stream and because they have no other means of coming to us but by a long land transportation through unimproved roads."

Even though America had defeated the British, they refused to move out of the western lands and so presented an ongoing danger to American settlers. A way was needed to join East and West.

The Potomac River, however, was difficult—185 miles of twisting water, most of which was unnavigable. Many men believed, however, that by building short canals, the obstacles could be overcome.

Washington was the prime mover. He was responsible for the formation of the Patowmack Company and of the James River Company. In the Spring of 1786, 200 laborers, indentured servants and slaves were at work on the Patowmack Company's project at the Great Falls. James Rumsey who had never seen a canal or a canal lock was put in charge. Immediately, problems arose. He could not control the men who fought and were drunk most of the time. In spite of problems, Rumsey had, by 1802, built five canals, the longest three, 814 feet, at the Little Falls. Washington died before this project was completed. The canals were a great help to flat boats drawing not over a foot of water but they certainly did not connect the Potomac with the Ohio.

Thomas Jefferson followed Washington as head of the Patowmack

Company. His dreams of internal improvements were similar to those of Washington. In addition, he was aware of the potential problems of the bituminous coal beds near Cumberland. So much time and money had been expended in blasting a channel through the rocky gorge south of Point of Rocks, 20 miles below Harpers Ferry, that the company was bankrupt. Appeals to the legislatures of Virginia and Maryland were to no avail. There were no buyers of new stock.

In November 1823, a canal convention was held in Washington. A few years earlier, General Simon Bernard, a famous French engineer, had estimated the cost of a canal from Georgetown to Pittsburgh to be the unheard of sum of $22,000,000. Nathan Roberts and James Geddes were called in to examine the report with the hopes of reducing the cost. They reported that the cost would be $11,000,000, still an impossible amount. This ended any talk of a canal across the mountains to Pittsburgh. The convention delegates turned their attention to a canal from Georgetown to Cumberland which Geddes and Roberts estimated to cost $4,000,000. The federal Government inserted its requirements that the proposed canal must be 60 feet wide at the surface and 6 feet deep which added materially to the cost; however, the Government pledged to invest $1,000,000. The convention recommended a subscription of $2,000,000.

The company was to be called the Chesapeake and Ohio Company (C. and O.). It was not until 1828 that sufficient subscriptions were secured to warrant the charter. Baltimore contributed nothing having found out that no branch canal from Point of Rocks to Baltimore would be built. Virginia became lukewarm when the survey showed the canal going up the Maryland side of the Potomac all the way. Other sources finally subscribed the minimum.

On July 4, 1828, a grand celebration was held with President John Q. Adams to dig the first shovel full of dirt. Progress was so slow that it took 22 years to complete the canal. On the same day, 40 miles away, Charles Carrol was laying the first stone of the Baltimore and Ohio Railroad, an ominous event from the future of canals.

Financial troubles dogged the C. and O. all the way. The company was in debt, its state bonds were going begging. Landowners along the route refused to give the company right of way at reasonable prices thus forcing the C. and O. to condemn almost the entire route to Point of Rocks and to pay exorbitant prices for the land. A cholera epidemic in 1832 caused the death of so many workers that the project was stopped for a long time.

In the meantime, the city of Alexandria, Virginia, realized that the only way it could be connected to the canal was by means of an aqueduct across the Potomac at Georgetown and an extension of the canal along the south shore of the river. The C. and O. company refused to consider such an expensive enterprise, so Alexandria with help from the federal government built it on its own. It was completed in 1833. This was for many years the only connection between the north and south shores of the river. During the Civil War, the north captured the aqueduct, drained off the water and converted it into a foot and wagon bridged. Over it marched thousands of men in blue, moving cannon and munitions with them.

On July 30, 1830, we find Roberts at Harpers Ferry Falls locating the route of the canal. Then he moved to Point of Rocks. Here he worked on the canal, but at the same time he worked on a route for the Baltimore and Ohio Railroad. Roberts' interests had broadened to include railroads—he was a man of vision. He could see that it was only a matter of time before the railroads would far surpass canals. He had previously been appointed a commissioner of the B. and O. under the Chancellor of Maryland and was associated with Jonathan Knight also a commissioner. Roberts' belief in the future of railroads is evidenced by the railroad stocks owned by him at the time of his death.

The competition between the canal and the newly formed railroad was sometimes ludicrous. When the canal finally reached Point of Rocks, it found the B. and O. already there. At this place, the narrow shelf of land between the cliffs and the river was not wide enough to allow both canal and railroad to go through. The railroad claimed the right of way. The C. and O. appealed to the courts claiming prior rights and won. Not to be outdone, the B. and O. built a tunnel through the mountain at Point of Rocks. Then the canal and the railroad ran side aby side along the river with only a fence, built under court order by the B. and O. to separate them. At their destination, Cumberland, the respective crews pelted each other with rocks. The B. and O. engineer enjoyed blasting the train whistles to stampede the horses on the towpath.

Roberts and his party returned to Georgetown on July 4, 1831 to turn in their reports to the canal company. He was directed to report to the Chancellor at Annapolis. His comment on the condition of Annapolis at this time is of interest:

"This ancient city is much on the decline. The old state house is yet in tolerable repair, where Gen. George Washington resigned his commission to Congress and from which he retired to private life at Mount Vernon in Virginia on the west bank of the Potomac about twelve miles down the river from the city of Washington."

Roberts spent a week in Annapolis seeing the sights and making new friends. He returned to Washington in August. During the following fall and winter he worked on the first division of the C. and O. canal and on the canal from Georgetown to Alexandria. He also worked on the city canal, a canal from the city of Georgetown upon the high level to the navy yard for the purpose of a dry dock, for hydraulic power and for supplying the city with water to extinguish fires. In early 1931, he had completed a canal from Georgetown to Point of Rocks, a distance of 48 miles.

At this time, the suit concerning the priority of the right of way between the canal and the railroad was pending before the Chancellor of Maryland. The final result of the suit seemed to Roberts to be far in the future. In the meantime, his work could not be continued. He reported to the Board saying that the service he could render them under the circumstances was small, so he resigned and returned home on April 20th. This was only a few days previous to the great political explosion which took place in Washington. Van Buren and Eaton resigned and President Andrew Jackson fired the remainder of the cabinet. Roberts was sorry he had not waited a while longer to leave Washington, for, although he monitored the events from home as well as he could, to have been in Washington at the time would have been exciting. Roberts was a loyal Jacksonian Democrat and was intensely interested in politics. Had his profession   allowed him to remain in one place for any length of time, he might well have run for office.

What a homecoming it must have been. Roberts had not been home for two years. The children had, of course, grown unbelievably. DeWitt was now fourteen, old enough to be a great help to his mother on the farm. Mary Jane, twelve, was a little mother to France Josephine, now four, and to Lavinia Catherine, six. Albert, at nine, surely had chores to do as well.

To Lavinia, the return of her husband must have afforded immeasurable relief. Although half of the one thousand acre farm was leased on shares, the total responsibility for management fell on her shoulders. She should have known, however, that such relief would not last for long. Roberts had been home for less than two months when John Boardman, Secretary of the Tennessee Canal came to the Roberts' home in Lenox to deliver an invitation to Roberts to visit Muscle Shoals in Alabama to do a feasibility study of a proposed canal there. After three days deliberation during which Lavinia and the children protested loud and long the lure of canal construction won out. He reassured the family that it would only take two weeks. Roberts surely knew that this was not accurate as it was impossible to get to Alabama in two weeks. He arranged his affairs so that Lavinia could more conveniently take care of the farm. He made arrangements for the further education of the children. He definitely felt some qualms as he noted that he had never been so far from home before.

A few days before Roberts left, Margaret White, Lavinia's sister, was married at the Roberts' home to John Crouse, merchant of Canastota. As the bride descended the beautiful stairway, she had the not unusual qualms which beset brides. This had been her home for seven years. Lavinia had been more a mother to her than her own. Although she was only moving a mile away and although she loved John dearly, it was to be a whole new life, different from the bucolic one on the fairly isolated Roberts' farm. Now she was to be a village wife living in the beautiful new house John had built on Peterboro Street only a half block from his store and from the bustle of the Canal.

Lavinia was indeed bereft. Not only was her husband going away, but this younger sister had, since 1824, been her companion and confidante. She had been present for the births of Lavinia Catherine and of Frances Josephine. Even though, Margaret would only be a mile away, Lavinia knew that her home responsibilities would now allow frequent visits.

John Crouse and his brother, Daniel, operated one of the first grocery stores on the Erie Canal for seventeen years. Then John and Margaret moved to Syracuse where John dealt in wholesale groceries and became a millionaire. In 1887, Syracuse University was in dire need of a building for its fine arts program which was encroaching on space intended for liberal arts. John Crouse, then wealthy enough to be called the Honorable John Crouse, merchant and banker, was approached and enthusiastically consented to donate a building to be known as the "John Crouse Memorial Building for Women" in memory of his wife, Margaret. The building was erected under the direct supervision of Crouse who moved in with his own architect, masons, and carpenters. The building was almost complete when on June 27, 1889, Crouse died; however, immediately, his son, D. Edgar Crouse, assumed the completion of the building according to his father's wishes that it be a "memorial college for women" (as is evident from the inscription over the entrance to the building). The building was never used exclusively for women but quickly became known as the College of Fine Arts. It is now called the Crouse College of Music.

The building was constructed of Long Meadow red sandstone, four stories high crowned by an imposing tower housing the Crouse chimes. Chancellor Sims declared it to be the finest college edifice in the world.

Crouse College is still probably the most beautiful building in the city as it stands on the highest elevation of the University campus overlooking the city. It is listed in the National Register of Historic Buildings in America.

14

Florence, Alabama

On June 18, Nathan Roberts left for his "two weeks" trip to Florence, Alabama. Herein is an account of the distances and expenses of traveling from Lenox, Madison County, to Florence, Alabama as recorded in Roberts' journal.

June 18th,	Packet boat to Rochester - 124 miles	$ 4.96
" 20th,	Breakfast at Rochester	.38
" 20th,	Packet to Buffalo - 94 miles	3.75
" 21st,	One day and overnight at Buffalo	1.00
	Postage, etc.	.25
" 22nd,	Steamboat Enterprise	
	Capt. Miles for Sandusky, distance about 250 miles	
	Driven by head winds and missed stage	
	Stop one day at Sandusky	1.12½
" 25th,	Stage to Columbus, 112 miles	5.75
	Stage to Dayton, 60 miles	3.75
	From Sandusky dinner and supper and passing	
	overnight at Mount Vernon and breakfast	1.00
" 26th,	At Columbus	
	From Columbus. Dine at Darby Plains	.37½
	Overnight at Springfield	.50
" 27th,	Breakfast at Dayton	.37½
	Expense from home to Dayton, 640 miles	29.95
" 27th,	Passage in canal packet boat from Dayton	
	to Cincinnati, 65 miles	2.50
" 28th,	In the morn, arrived at Cincinnati. Detained	
	one day for steamboat.	
" 29th,	Expense at Cincinnati	1.69½
	Largest city above New Orleans 30,000 inhabitants	
" 29th,	Wednesday took passage for Louisville in steamboat.	
	Magnolia, 150 miles	4.00
	Returned for stage at Louisville, Kentucky	
	10,000 inhabitants	1.37½
July 1st,	Stage fare to Nashville, 180 miles	12.00
	Breakfast	.37½

	Pass Elizabeth, dinner	.37½
" 2nd,	Overnight Houghton	.50
	Breakfast at Bacon Creek	.37½
	Pass Mumfordville	
	Dinner at Bells	.37½
July 3rd,	Sunday expense at Bowling Green, Ky.	1.50
" 4th,	Monday breakfast at Franklin Courthouse	.37½
	Dine at Spring Tavern	.50
	Overnight at capital of Tennessee	
	Nashville, 5000 inhabitants, 110 miles	.65
		8.75
July 5th,	Breakfast	.37½
	Dinner	.50
	Supper and lodging at Mt. Pleasant	.50
" 6th,	Breakfast at Simington	.40
	Dinner at State Line	.25
	Thence to Florence Eagle Hotel	
	Total distance 1145 miles	1.
	Expenses	$66.70

Roberts commented on the territory he covered:

"From Lenox to Buffalo the canal passes many flourishing villages most of which were intensely blank woods, and but a few had commenced at all when I assisted in locating the canal in the years 1817-1823. Among the latter was Syracuse, Clyde, then called Block House, Lyons, Palmyra, Pittsford, Rochester and Buffalo. Most of the others, at present numerous and flourishing were then without a name and most of them from Buffalo to Sandusky were not seen. The lake is 30 to 100 miles wide and we often met steamboats and passed schools without a house. From Sandusky city across the state of Ohio the country resembles in its soil, its villages, improvement and products the western parts of New York.

The Ohio River at Cincinnati is about half as wide as from Cincinnati to Louisville and pursuing the stage route from there to Florence the state of Kentucky is mostly second rate land and Tennessee appears much better to the south line at Alabama. From there the 18 miles to Florence may be mostly considered as second rate though pleasant land.

An approximation of the population of some of the principal towns passed through in the preceding journey, viz.:

Rochester	12,000
Buffalo	8,000
Cleveland, Ohio	2,000

Sandusky	400
Mount Vernon	1,000
Columbus	2,000
Dayton	3,000
Cincinnati	30,000
Louisville	10,000
Nashville	5,000
Florence	1,300

So Roberts arrived at Florence, Alabama to face the next challenge of his engineering career. The Tennessee River descended here in a series of rapids called Muscle Shoals, more than thirty-five miles long with a drop of more than one hundred and thirty feet. The river was at this location completely unnavigable. It was Roberts' job to determine whether or not this obstacle could be bypassed by a canal. Roberts immediately got to work on the problem.

All, however, was not work. Among other things, he attended a barbecue given by an Irish gentleman named James Jackson. As Roberts tells us,

> "A barbecue is called a sylvan feast and consists of a public dinner served with good wine and brandy in a natural grove of forest trees near a fine stream or spring evidently something like a Madison County clam bake. The gentlemen of the neighborhood and for some distance around are invited and all are entertained for free. Sometimes the feasts are of a political nature, in which candidates for office appear and deliver their sentiments in what is termed a stump speech. It is probable that the origin of the word 'stump' came from the speeches being made at these barbecues from a tree stump."

Roberts noted that there was an abundance of deer and that wild turkeys, foxes and grey squirrels were often hunted by sportsmen. Kentucky already had the reputation of raising superior cattle and horses.

He found the style of living to be very different from that to which he was accustomed. The reason for the wide difference he traced to slavery. He considered the farmers in Alabama, instead of being the most industrious and economical to be the laziest and most indolent, often the more so as the number of their slaves increased. The labor was all done by slaves directed for the most part by an overseer. The farmer and his family throw as much business to their hands as possible, even the cooking was performed by a slave to relieve the master and mistress of all drudgery. The style of cooking was very indifferent, as it was very ungenteel for the mistress of the house to meddle with such matters. The taste of the black females was the standard of cookery in all the best and most opulent houses. The quality of their cooking, baking, washing, bedding and furniture was far inferior to that enjoyed by northern farmers and merchants who had one fourth the wealth.

It is obvious that Mr. Roberts was not in love with the south. For a man whose house was reputed to be a link in the underground railway, the existence of slavery was appalling.

The Muscle Shoals Canal which Roberts planned during the first year extended along the Tennessee River for fourteen and one-quarter miles. The lockage was to be one hundred and three feet, divided into sixteen lift locks, besides two guard locks. The whole length of the canal would be about thirty-six miles extending from Florence Ferry to Brown Ferry and would improve the Tennessee River so that navigation would be good for boats of one hundred tons as far as Knoxville which is located more than two hundred miles to the east.

The canal commissioners prevailed upon Roberts to remain and to superintend the construction of the works as engineer-in-chief. He protested at first, because he was so far from home and family, and because the southern climate did not agree with his health. At length he was prevailed upon to accept the appointment and remain in Florence during the winter of 1831 until February 22, 1932.

On that day, he set out on horseback to visit his home in Canastota. Horseback was the only practical way to go as the waterways were for the most part frozen at that time of the year, and most stages were not running. He made the trip of approximately a thousand miles in twenty-seven days, an outstanding feat for a man in his late fifties. Roberts visited the great Natural Bridge in Virginia for several hours, but for the most part he rode straight on, reaching home on March 25.

His summary of the trip is as follows:

> From Florence to Huntsville - 70 miles
> From Huntsville to Knoxville, Tennessee - 208 miles
> From Knoxville to Abington, Virginia - 134 miles
> From Abington to Wythe Court House - 56 miles
> From Wythe to Staunton - 166 miles
> From Staunton to Winchester - 96 miles
> From Winchester to Willamsport - 35 miles
> From Willamsport to Hagerstown - 6 miles
> From Hagerstown to Pennsylvania - 8 miles

> From State Line to Chambersburg - 12 miles
> From Chambersburg to Harrisburg - 48 miles
> From Harrisburg to Montrose - 165 miles
> From Montrose to Chenango Point - 40 miles
> From Chenango Point to Binghamton to Oxford - 36 miles
> From Oxford to Hamilton - 40 miles
> From Hamilton to Lenox 20 miles
> Making the whole distance 1139 miles from Florence,
> 27 days traveling equals 31 miles per day.

(Note: Obviously there is a mathematical discrepancy here. Thirty-one miles a day for twenty-seven days would be eight hundred and thirty-seven miles. It is inconceivable that Roberts, an engineer, could have made such an obvious error. The mistake must have come in the transcription by Smith. It is true, however, that Roberts did make the trip by horseback arriving home on March 25th. If he was in the saddle every day of the elapsed thirty-two he would have averaged thirty-five miles per day.)

The expense from beginning to end was about $1.12½ per day, amounting to $41.62½.

Robert s comments that the trip was very hard on the horses as a quarter of the way was in deep mud. As he approached familiar territory, he made the following comments:

> "From Morrisville to Peterboro is about five miles and in this distance is the summit dividing the waters of the Chesapeake Bay for those which run northwardly into the Mohawk. Five or six miles farther north, the waters run into Lake Ontario and thence into the St. Lawrence. This dividing ridge is valuable land of limestone and its attendant fertility. This partakes very much of the same quality of soil found in the great western country in the state of New York known to be so excellent for the finest crops of wheat, corn, oats, rye, and for all purposes of grazing and agriculture. About nine miles from Peterboro my place of residence is situated on the great Seneca Turnpike road and in the vicinity of the grand Erie Canal. I think it is a delightful situation, the soil is excellent and the location valuable."

Once again, he is impressed with the growth of Canastota:

> "The Village of Canastota on the canal is growing in commercial advantages and is a beautiful situation for a town. It accommodates the country for a distance of twenty or thirty miles in circumference and the leading roads are well located to insure to it and the adjacent country

great convenience and mutual commercial advantages which will increase in proportion to their respective wealth and population. The Village of Canastota is situated on what was denominated the Canastota
Reservation, and when the canal was located in 1816, it contained of
only two small houses and two or three Indian cabins or wigwams. It
now (1832) contains four dry goods stores, six or eight groceries and a
number of machine shops, etc. besides some handsome private
dwellings. It contains probably about three hundred inhabitants."

At home, Roberts found that two of the children were away. DeWitt
had been at the Hamilton Academy since December and Mary Jane was
attending school in Whitesboro and living with her grandmother. The
other children attended the district school, taught by a Mr. Foran with
whom Roberts was pleased. The winter had been very cold and although
the stock had an abundance of hay, the Roberts farm suffered a loss of
nearly one-fourth of the cattle and one third of the sheep.

Roberts spent the months of April and May and part of June at home
and enjoyed every minute of it. One part of him really wanted to be a
farmer. He built fences and drained and ditched wet places on the farm.
He planned a road to the lake. He planted a nursery of locust trees with
seeds he had brought from Alabama. He built an eighty-foot shed on the
north side of the barn. Most enjoyable of all was the fact that before he
left again, all the children were back at home. He decided to let DeWitt
stay home for a while and to work the farm and made arrangements for
Mary Jane to go to Hamilton Academy in July or August.

This was the time of great religious fervor in Central New York
which later caused the area to be called the "Burned Over District."
Roberts comments on the religious excitement which existed in Canastota
when the Methodists and Presbyterians held revival meetings sometimes
for as long as two weeks. Roberts was a member of the Presbyterian
(formerly Dutch Reformed) Church. He always contributed to the church
and attended the regular services; however, it is doubtful that he attended
the revival meetings as any outward show of emotion was foreign to him.
He seemed to disapprove of the Presbyterian Church's dismissal of Reverend Olds who had preached at the church for twenty years and seemed
a very worthy citizen.

Roberts in commenting on the Panic of 1831 said that

"Many of the public works were suspended in different states, and
the banks nearly all stopped payment. Over-importing by merchants,
over-buying for country merchants and over-banking by speculators,

and over-issuing and discounting by most of the banks and over-trading in public lands and other real estate, has had all the bad effects that might have been apprehended, though most of the farmers were not led into these wild speculations, and laid up their money, and when others were receiving the reward of extravagance and folly, the prudent farmer was now at ease on his farm, employed in his economical labors as usual."

On June 13, 1832, Roberts left for his last season in Alabama. What had begun as a two week project would take up the better part of three years. On this trip, he took a slightly different route whether for convenience or from his curiosity to see as much of the country as possible is not know. At Maysville, Ohio, he stopped for a couple of days to visit his brother-in-law, Halsey White who had resided there for twelve years.

This final season was uneventful with an exceptionally mild winter. There was considerable sickness among the workers but not more than Roberts had experience on the Erie. Even in this remote area, Roberts still kept up his interest in politics. He hailed with joy the election of Andrew Jackson and the defeat of all "Antis," especially in the Anti-Masons.

With his work completed, Roberts gratefully started for his home on March 24, 1833. He left Florence by steamer for Louisville, a distance of six hundred miles by the Tennessee and Ohio Rivers. Even in the three years spent by Roberts in Alabama, we can see a vast improvement in public transportation. He stopped at Cincinnati, the largest city in the west. Once again he spent time with Halsey White. From Maysville, he took a steamer for three hundred and fifty miles to Wheeling.

On April 6, he left Wheeling and by traveling day and night, he reached Frederick Maryland in three days. From Frederick, he took the B. and O. Railroad to Baltimore, a distance of sixty miles traveling at about twenty miles an hour. A quick visit to Washington on business consumed two days. Between Baltimore and Philadelphia he rode on the French-town and New Castle railroad drawn by steam locomotives at the rate of eighteen to twenty miles an hour. He found this to be a delightful ride on an almost straight road. On the way to New York, he rode from Borden-town to Amboy, one hundred and thirty-five miles on the railroad across New Jersey, drawn by horses at a rate of about ten miles an hour.

On April 12, he arrived in New York City were he stayed at Niblo's Congress Hall. Roberts did not tarry long in the city; after buying a gold watch for Lavinia and earrings and a brooch for Mary Jane, he continued on to Albany. This trek was difficult as he traveled by steamboat with about five hundred other passengers and "had neither bed nor mattress during the whole night."

In Albany he met with Commissioners Bouck and Earl. Roberts and Bouck, later Governor of New York, had been friends for years. During the construction of the Erie Canal when Bouck was a Canal Commissioner and Roberts an engineer, they had corresponded frequently concerning Canal problems. Although we are not sure what the men discussed, it is logical to assume in light of ensuing events, that the conversation centered around the enlargement of the Erie Canal.

At nine o'clock, on the fourteenth, Roberts left Albany in a railroad car, on the Mohawk and Hudson, drawn by two horses. Although impatient to get home he was detained for a day at Schenectady because the stage was full and the canal not yet opened for the season. On the seventeenth, he arrived at his home. He was delighted to see his new son, Nathan S. Roberts, Jr., who had been born on the fourth of February.

Roberts had taken home with him about four thousand dollars out of which he paid his hired man, paid tuition for the schooling of three children, donated one hundred fifty dollars toward the new church, paid seventy-two dollars tax to a new schoolhouse and lent out one thousand five hundred dollars on bond and mortgage security. He also bought some land as follows:

$700 for Lively Place	44 acres
$40 for Foote Place	30 acres
$450 for saw mill and lot	14 acres
$350 for part of lot 86	12 acres

From this time until the spring of 1835, Roberts stayed at home. Except for consultations with engineers who came to the home for advice, he spent the time farming and improving his holdings. In the latter part of the period, he drew the plans for the enlargement of the Erie Canal.

15

THE ENLARGEMENT OF THE ERIE

The Erie Canal was hardly completed in 1825 before the need for widening and deepening the channel became obvious. No one in his wildest dreams anticipated that the one hundred sixty freight boats traveling the canal in 1826 would increase to three thousand by 1836. The profit to the state in 1826 was a million dollars and by 1836 the remaining debt of three and a half million was paid off.

Traffic snarls with ensuing fights were the rule of the day. Packet-boats racing along as fast as seven miles an hour were tearing down the walls of the canal. The imposition of a four mile an hour speed limit did little to improve the situation since many captains preferred to pay the fine rather than to slow down.

In the summer and fall of 1834, Roberts carefully made surveys and reports on the enlargement of the canal. His proposals were as follows:

> Width - top water line - 70 feet
> Width - bottom - 42 feet
> Depth - 7 feet
> Length of locks between gates - 110 feet
> Width chamber lock - 180 feet
> Rochester acqueduct [sic] waterway - 45 feet with 7 arches of
> 52 feet span on 10 ft. rises

In addition, in many places double locks were to be installed in place of single ones. The route of the canal was to be changed in some areas necessitating the building of whole new sections. An example of this was at Rome. "The original Erie Canal ran through the swamp far enough to the south of Rome for it to be necessary to build a crude turnpike to the town through a quagmire. The decision was to cut through the summit of the divide between the Hudson and Oswego water systems, where Rome stands, in order to obtain a single water level from New London to Caseys' Corners. The change placed the relocated canal through the north edge of the swamp some ten feet lower than the original Erie Canal and several feet below the water level of the swamp."

As can be seen, the task facing Nathan Roberts was enormous; however, he approached it with his usual calm efficiency.

On Roberts' fifty-ninth birthday, March 18, 1835, we find him at the Monroe House in Rochester. This was to be his winter home for most of the next five years. As the Rochester aqueduct was the most complicated problem of the enlargement, he decided to make Rochester his headquarters. Rochester, in 1835, would not have been recognized by a traveler as the village of Rochesterville as seen in 1817 before the Erie was accessible. Wheat production in the area was mounting rapidly, and there were several mills in operation; however, the Canadian market was the only one available to the wheat growers of the time, although the route there was not ideal because of poor transportation facilities and the frozen St. Lawrence River. By 1822, Rochester had half a dozen mills and three thousand one hundred residents. "When the 1823 shipping season opened, there was such a demand for the product in the east that the first ten shipping days saw 10,450 barrels of flour begin their journey to Albany and New York City aboard fifty-eight canal boats." At the peak of production, Rochester had thirty-one mills producing a million barrels of flour yearly. Ironically, the Erie Canal which had made Rochester the breadbasket of America, was ultimately responsible for removing it to the west as travelers covered the whole route and settled on the fertile lands of the then far west.

The original aqueduct had taken two years and three thousand dollars to build and had been considered an engineering wonder and thing of beauty in 1823. It was the longest stone arch bridge in America, eight hundred four feet in length. The supports were nine, fifty foot Roman arches with two smaller arches at each end. The walls of Medina sandstone were accented by a coping of gray limestone The piers were sunk into the bedrock to a depth of at least half a foot and iron clamps were fitted into the holes drilled in the large stone slabs that made up the piers and arches with bolts holding the masonry together; however, serious flaws soon became evident. Boats on the west side of the river were required to make a right angle turn onto the aqueduct. Also the span was only seventeen feet wide which meant that only one boat could cross at a time. Boatmen fought over the turn and over the right of passage. More important, the narrow width of the aqueduct restricted the flow of water needed for the canal. The sandstone blocks of the foundation were crumbling and there was a tendency for the whole structure to leak.

The new aqueduct was more pretentious and more practical than the old. It was eight hundred forty-eight feet long and forty-five feet wide, made mainly of Syracuse limestone. It was a beautiful sight. The final touches were not completed until 1842.

During the years when Roberts worked in Rochester, he was able to spend part of the winter months at home, a treat for him and for his family. On March 18, 1836, he spent his sixtieth birthday at home. All the children except DeWitt, now nineteen and a student at Hamilton College, were at home for the celebration. Mary Jane, seventeen, had returned from her studies at Cazenovia Seminary the previous day. The previous winter had been a rough one, the coldest and snowiest since 1806, the year of the great eclipse. Snow had been four to five feet deep on the level for weeks. As late as March 27, it was still two feet deep and crusted. For the younger children, so much snow must have been a treat, but for Nathan and Albert, who was a great help to his father, it was a grim battle against the elements. Simply keeping a path open to the barn, which was located two hundred feet from the house, was a daily chore. Roads were blocked but fortunately there was an abundant supply of food for the animals in the barn. In spite of their efforts, Roberts lost two fine colts and thirty sheep.

As a result of the severe winter, the summer wheat crop was small, causing prices to rise from $1.75 to $2.00. Flour cost $10 and $11 a barrel. Prices continued to rise in 1837:

flour, $15
turkeys, 25¢ a lb. - $2 to $3 a pair
beef, 12½ a lb.
corned beef, 10¢ a lb.
mutton, 17-19¢ a lb.
veal, 18¢ a lb.
chickens, pair $2
potatoes, $1 bushel
pork, $22 a barrel

During the next two years, Roberts spent most of his time in Rochester working on the aqueduct. Usually he returned home in December for several months when the canal was frozen and work had to stop because of the cold. He made a number of trips to oversee other aspects of the work of enlarging the canal.

The year 1839 was a combination of work in Rochester and of personal affairs. One problem of the aqueduct was the inability of local contractors to carry out the detailed plans given to them by Roberts. New contractors, Kasson and Brown, were hired and put in charge of the excavation for the foundation of the new aqueduct by deepening the bed of the rock and most of the riverbed. The west mill dam had been built the spring before. Mr. William Buel, contractor, was put in charge of removing the rock for the foundation of the aqueduct. This work proceeded during the summer.

In June, Roberts returned home to attend two events. The Syracuse and Utica railroad was opened to the public on July 2. In the year 1839 however, Roberts had already had a trial run on it from Utica to Canastota on the twenty-ninth of June. Roberts was fascinated by railroads and I imagine had he been a younger man at this time, his career would have turned to the construction of railroads.

On the second of July, his oldest daughter, Mary Jane, was married to Israel Spencer, a young Canastota attorney. The ceremony was performed by the Reverend Mr. Van Sandwood. Mary Jane had received her higher education at Cazenovia Seminary, one of the stronger institutions of learning for young ladies in Central New York. Roberts felt that the education of women was as important as for men, and he tried most of the surrounding institutions in search of opportunities for his daughters.

During this visit, Roberts took Lavinia by carriage to see Colonel Angel DeFerrier's monument which had been erected in his memory at the DeFerrier home in Wampsville, a distance of two miles from the Roberts' home. DeFerrier was a wealthy French emigre who came to this area with Linklaen to found the village of Cazenovia. On the way, the party stopped at an inn in Wampsville where DeFerrier fell in love with an Indian princess. Later, he returned and married her.

The monument was a plain shaft of polished marble. Later, Lavinia saw a similar stone dedicated to Captain Timothy Brown. Perhaps these two monuments influenced Lavinia when she was required to choose a monument for her husband, as his stone is almost identical.

In August, DeWitt, the oldest son, graduated from Union College. DeWitt followed in his father's footsteps becoming an assistant engineer working on the enlargement of the canal. In addition to his formal education, he had been with his father on a number of jobs, receiving instruction from a great engineer.

In September, Roberts was back on the job in Rochester. On the twenty-seventh, he had two visitors, Russian engineers Colonel Milnekoff and Colonel Kroeff bearing introductory letters from the comptroller and from Mr. Ruggles, Commissioner.

The seven arches of the aqueduct were closed in September, and the men ceased laying masonry in mortar or granite on October 15; however, with the exception of a few days in late November when the canal was frozen, the weather remained mild. Eighty or ninety men worked on into December laying spandrel work dry (specialized masonry done on the arches) and in filling down the water tables. The dry work was to be set in mortar and grouted in the spring.

Some time during 1839, Roberts had his portrait painted by Grove Gilbert, a well-known upstate artist. For years the portrait hung at the top of the "Million Dollar Staircase" in Albany. Recently is has been on loan to the Canal Museum in Canastota. Grove was a member of the highly rated National Academy of Design, and his portraits were held in high esteem. It may well have been that Roberts was previously acquainted with Gilbert as the artist was a native of Clinton. The cost of the portrait was forty dollars and twelve dollars for the frame.

On the last day of the year, Roberts comments on the three feet of snow in Rochester. Although the canal was open from December 15 to December 25, we have no record of Roberts having gone home for Christmas. Albert and daughter Lavinia were at Hamilton Academy for the year, Albert in a collegiate course and Lavinia getting a "good competent education for a lady. Josephine, fourteen, and Smith, eight, were considered too young to be sent away from home.

Roberts must have been aware of things to come. He comments on great political changes taking place. The Democrats, although winning in 1836, were weakened by the fiscal policies of Jackson and Van Buren. The Whigs in 1837 nominated William Seward for governor. When the "bank" Democrats endorsed him over the Democratic candidate, Marcy, his election was assured. Roberts lists those elected as:

> Governor - Seward
> Lt. Governor - Bordick
> Secretary of State - L. Spencer
> Comptroller - Cook
> Surveyor - Orville Holley
> Treasurer - Gen. Haight
> Attorney General - William Hall

In 1839, the Democrats lost control of the Senate for the first time in two decades. The old canal commissioners—William C. Bouck, Jonas Cull, Jr., Samuel Yarney, William Baker, John Bowman—were all removed. They were replaced by Samuel Ruggles, Asa Whitney, Henry

16

CHANGES

Eighteen forty was a year of turmoil, tragedy and disappointment for Nathan Roberts. The new Canal Board, all Whigs, came early in 1840 to inspect Roberts' work at Rochester. They were all highly complimentary, expressing awe and wonder at his expertise. Roberts found them to be

> " . . . wanting in experience, governed by selfish political motives and not calculated to raise the reputation of the engineer department, as a scientific corp, nor the character of the Erie Canal improvement. They are aristocratic and political in their measures throughout. Their names will be long remembered for their federal and aristocratic management of the canal office."

In spite of Roberts' opinion of the new commissioners, he went along happily in his work. Commissioners, in the past, had never interfered with his work, and the group had seemed pleased with what he had done. By March, the seven arches had all been closed and the spandrels raised nearly to the crown of the arches.

On April 14, tragedy struck. Roberts was called home by the death of Mary Jane, twenty-one, who had married Israel Spencer less than a year before. She died suddenly in childbirth; Roberts was stunned. This was the first death in his family. As he expressed his grief,

> "This was more affecting owing to her situation, and the sudden and unexpected news was extremely grievous to bear—she had endeared herself to her parents and brothers and sisters and to her husband —and also to all her acquaintances, which for one of her age was quite extensive."

A large crowd attended the funeral held on April 17 at the Dutch Reformed Church in Canastota. The Reverend Mr. White conducted the service choosing as his text, "Boast not of tomorrow, for thou knowest not what a day may bring forth." Mary Jane was buried in the Quality Hill (Lenox Rural) Cemetery, a mile west of her home.

Eleven days later, Roberts returned to Rochester and to work. On July 6, 1840, the Canal Commissioners in Albany passed a resolution dispensing with his services as chief engineer. Roberts was shocked. He had had no hint that this might happen even though he was a member of a party in opposition to those in power in Albany. He thought of engineering as a professional job not subject to the machinations of politics. Immediately, a petition signed by one hundred eighty-five people requesting his reinstatement was circulated but to no avail. Politics had won out over efficiency.

On October 1, Roberts left the services of the State after tying up his affairs. He arrived at his home on October 5. Surely the family was overjoyed to have Roberts at home; however, he must have been depressed at the lack of recognition for all the years of service. Although he could have afforded a life of leisure, the idea never occurred to him. He immediately set to work to improve his farm and stock.

The family was smaller now with only Josephine, fourteen, and Smith, eight, at home. DeWitt, twenty-four, was still working as an assistant engineer on the Erie. Albert was a freshman at Hamilton College. Lavinia Catherine, now nineteen, was at Hamilton Academy, a very old school which later became Hamilton Female Seminary.

On his birthday each year, Roberts took stock of himself, his family, the weather, the state of the state and the nation. On March 18, 1842, Roberts, now sixty-six, saw his first robin which seemed a good omen for the year. The winter past had been the mildest ever known even to the oldest inhabitants. Early in March, it had been possible for him to begin to plow on his land south of the turnpike. Plowing continued every day from the fourth to the ninth with two plows in action.

Seward was Governor of New York and even though there was a Democratic majority in the Assembly and a majority of two in the Senate, Roberts felt that the Whigs had put the state so much in debt that a tax of a mill on the dollar must be imposed.

All members of the family were in good health. At home we find only Frances Josephine, who had been in Oneida the previous summer being taught by Miss Hitchcock, and young Nathan, who was still being taught at home. Lavinia was in school in Rochester but was expected home soon.

Roberts owned a large tract of land east of the village's main thoroughfare, Peterboro Street, and north of the canal. In April, he laid out the first street, four rods wide, in this section of the village. He also sold for two hundred twenty dollars the second lot east of the corner, sixty feet front and back and one hundred twenty feet deep. The villagers called him Judge Roberts since he had been made a side judge of the Court of Common Pleas.

In November 1842, an event took place which gave Roberts jubilant satisfaction. William C. Bouck was elected governor of New York with a majority of twenty-two thousand votes over Luther Bradish, Whig candidate. Bouck had long been a friend to Roberts and had been dismissed form the Board of Canal Commissioners after twenty years service at the same time that Roberts had been terminated. Roberts summed up the situation when he reacted with, "The Locos have treed the old Federal coons. Good!"

On December 31, Roberts watched the New York arrive with his usual philosophical calm. The month had been newsworthy as the snowiest and coldest in history.

The heavy snows of December turned to a severe thaw in January followed by more snow. It was the middle of February before people could dig out the roads. This proved to be a labor of frustration since the winds picked up, drifting the snow, making the roads once again impassable or at best hazardous.

On Roberts' sixty-seventh birthday, he was still a rugged man. His only complaint was of partial deafness for the past two years. This might well have been the result of the years of blasting to which he had been subjected. A man who had spent a great deal of his life sleeping in tents, who had ridden horseback from Florence to Canastota and who had had only one serious illness must be considered an extremely lucky person. Of the original chief engineers on the Erie, Roberts and Charles Brodhead were the only two still living. Canvass White, Judge Geddes, Judge Bates and Judge Benjamin Wright were all dead. Of the Canal Commissioners who served between 1816 and 1825, Ephraim Hart, General Van Rensselaer, Henry Seymour, Myron Holley and DeWitt Clinton were all gone. Only Governor Bouck remained.

March 1843 went out like a lion with three feet of snow on the ground, and all north and south roads closed. On April 1, there was a heavy snowstorm accompanied by high winds. Not until May 15 did the apple blossoms begin to bloom.

The year 1844 brought another tragedy to the Roberts with the death of DeWitt's wife. DeWitt returned home bringing with him his baby daughter, Caroline Victoria, born on June 16, 1843. The baby must have been a welcome addition, for Lavinia and Nathan had not had a baby in the home for quite a while. Even after DeWitt subsequently married

Helen Ward of Manlius, Caroline continued to make her home with the Roberts. Grandpa Nathan described her as a "promising child."

Albert, at this time, was a senior at Union College and Frances Josephine was at Utica Ladies' Seminary. DeWitt, Lavinia and Smith were not at home. DeWitt had been studying law for a year and a half and helped his father on the farm. The year was a good one on the farm with much more favorable weather than the previous winter.

On May 22 Roberts left home for Baltimore. He had been appointed the previous September a delegate from the 22nd Congressional District of New York to the Congressional Convention for the nomination of the President with instructions to vote for Martin Van Buren. The instructions fitted well with Roberts' political views. He was in favor of an independent treasury and against the lending of the national revenue to corporations for the purpose of political speculators in a national bank.

Roberts' description of the meeting follows.

> The 23rd we all met in New York at the Astor House and from there adjourned to meet in Baltimore on Saturday evening, 25th May, where we were all (36 in number) present on Monday, 27th, at 11 o'clock. The whole delegation, 266 in number assembled at the splendid building called Odd Fellows Hall, in the Egyptian saloon, and after various conversings, we found that we must abandon our most favorite candidate for the sake of harmony, as in Democratic principles we were all agreed but not in men. It was therefore agreed on the second or third day, after seven ballotings, that we must withdraw our favorite and all other states did the same. After teh eighth balloting, Governor James K. Polk of Tennessee, was presented to the convention and after the second balloting, he was unanimously chosen as candidate for the office of President of the United States. Silas Wright, our United States Senator, was then chosen by 266 votes for candidate for Vice President which he totally declined, and on Thursday morning, the 30th or May, after two or three ballotings, the honorable George M. Dalles of Pennsylvania was chosen unanimously as our candidate for Vice President, and at about 8 o'clock the convention adjourned. The greatest harmony prevailed throughout, and the candidates were endorsed throughout the country. I was absent [from home] eleven days and the expense was about $50, but the satisfaction was a delightful compensation, as the nomination appears to be very popular with the Democratic party throughout the country. I arrived at home on Saturday evening, 1st of June, 1844, in sound health, and no accidents happened during the whole setting of this splendid convention."

Van Buren had lost the nomination because of his stand on the question of the annexation of Texas. Most Democrats took the position that if the people of Texas wanted to join the Union, they could do so without the consent of Mexico. Polk's inaugural address was delivered at ten o'clock, March 4, 1845 and received by Roberts in Canastota in forty-eight hours from Washington. Roberts was pleased with Polk and with his cabinet. Texas had been annexed even before Polk's inauguration.

The last entry in Roberts' journal was on his seventieth birthday, March 18, 1846, when he comments on his usual good health and on the prosperity of his farm. All the children were at home for his birthday except Albert, a law student at Hamilton. There is no hint that he intended to discontinue his journal; however, it may be guessed that he had decided to write his memoirs. A two-volume edition of his memoirs was written and published. Unfortunately the author has been unable to find a copy of this work. Roberts lived for another five years after the last entry in the journal.

He died on November 24, 1851 and was buried in Lenox Rural Cemetery in the family plot. His stone is s simple marble shaft similar to, but not as tall as that which memorializes Angel DeFerrier in Wampsville. It bears the following inscription:

> Sacred to the memory of Nathan S. Roberts
> who died November 24, 1851, in the 76th
> year of his age. He was born at Piles Grove,
> New Jersey on the 28th of March, 1776.
>
> Made poor by the war of the Revolution,
> in which his father served. He raised himself
> by his extraordinary talents and integrity
> from a humble condition, and became one of
> the most eminent Civil Engineers of the age.
> This marble has been erected over his remains
> by his affectionate wife and children who
> revered his virtues; but his noblest monuments
> are to be found amongst the great
> public works of his country.

17

Nathan's Will

Nathan Roberts succeeded in his determination that his family would never suffer the grinding poverty which he had known as a young man. Even in death, he left his wife and children well cared for.

Provision of his will are as follows:

To Lavinia: $10,728.18

To each child: $4,291.28

In addition: To Lavinia, the use of the residence, furniture, farm stock, tools, etc. during the minority of Nathan, the youngest son.

To DeWitt: That portion of land on which he lives, east of the home farm—35 acres with buildings. In addition, Lot 46 (155½ acres) and the part of Lot 45 called the Stevens part (35 acres).

To Albert: The southerly part of the Canastota farm (across the Turnpike) on which he lives, 145 acres and buildings. Also the farm on the Erie Canal, 2½ miles west of Canastota (96 acres) and buildings.

To Lavinia Williams: The land in Lenox Basin known as the Blute Place and 26 acres of Lot 62 parallel to the Blute Place - total 187½ acres.

To Frances Josephine Fiske: Land totaling 184½ acres encompassing the Foot and Morrison Places. Also the eastern quarter of land south of the Turnpike.

To both daughters: To be divided, the remainder of the home farm west of Peterboro Street.

To Nathan: When his education is complete and he is twenty-one - that part of the home farm west of Peterboro Street and north of the Seneca Turnpike. Also the west part of the home farm on the south side of the Turnpike and all buildings. Also the saw mill on the Canastota Creek - total 230 acres.

To Lavinia: One part of money ($4,291.28) for the care of granddaughter, Caroline.

Stock—120 shares of Syracuse and Utica R.R.:
  60 shares to wife and Nathan
  60 shares - 6 parts - one to Caroline and one to each child.

To Nathan R. Williams (Grandson): gold watch, key and chain.

Library books: To be divided after Lavinia determines which Smith
  needs.

There seems to be some partiality shown toward Nathan Smith, the youngest son; however, this young man had not yet completed his education nor had he determined what his profession would be. The other children were well settled in their own homes, the sons established in professions and the daughters married.

In his parting tribute to his wife, he said:

"During the first twenty-four years of our married life, my public employed me to be absent for more than nine-tenths of the time and frequently more than a year at a time and left domestic business wholly to my worthy wife for her management. Thus we came up the hill of life together."

18

Lavinia's Will

Lavinia Roberts died on March 30, 1858, seven years after the death of Nathan Roberts. He had already distributed his land holdings, railroad stock, etc., therefore, Lavinia's will was a much simpler document. It read as follows:

To Albert: $6,000 for the following purposes - the interest to be paid semi-annually to Caroline for her lifetime or to the person with whom she lives.

To Albert: $1,000

To Nathan Smith Roberts: $2,000 and the covered carriage, covered sleigh and my library.

To Frances Fiske: $500

The balance of real and personal property to Israel Spencer for the following purposes: Interest semi-annually to Lavinia Williams during her life and at her death, half of the remaining estate to grandchild Nathan Roberts Williams. The interest on the other half to Frances Fiske and then to grandchild, William Fiske.

To daughters and granddaughter: silver and crystal.

Household furniture to be divided between Smith, Frances and Lavinia.

At the death of Caroline: The $6,000 (trust fund) shall go to Albert, Smith, Francis and Lavinia.

Vernon Mason (Canastota)
Mrs. Catherine Crouse (Syracuse)

AFTERWORD

Although the work ethic, undoubtedly inherited from his New England ancestors, was unusually strong in Nathan Roberts, it was not until he was over forty years old that he could be deemed a success. He worked hard, frequently changing jobs in an effort to better himself. After he had taught for more than twenty years, his teaching salary was only a dollar or two more than his starting salary. In his land speculations, he had acquired a farm, hardly more; however, when at forty, opportunity came his way, it was upward and onward all the way.

Although the public works to which Lavinia referred on his tombstone, with the exception of the Chesapeake and Delaware Canal, are mainly in ruins, Roberts made a valuable contribution to the history of America. To him, and to others like him who worked on the Erie, goes the credit for establishing the supremacy of New York City as America's finest port. Also the transportation of thousands of pioneers to the west gave to them a new life and a way east for their produce thus binding the nation together.

In his innovative engineering achievements on the Pennsylvania Main Line Canal, he once more provided a way west as was also true for the Chesapeake and Potomac. In Alabama, Roberts laid the groundwork and showed the possibilities of the area which would become the great TVA of a much later era providing electricity for several states.

Roberts was a man torn between his love and responsibility toward his family and his consuming ambition to achieve success in his field. Whenever he returned from an assignment he busied himself with affairs at home, improving his farm, consulting with his farm manager, enlarging his land holdings, taking care of financial matters, locating appropriate schools for the children, and discussing politics with his village acquaintances. He was always willing to use his expertise for the improvement of the village in matters such as roads, plans for the north side, and for the canal itself. There was always, however, the lure of the canal building, the challenges to be met and the knowledge that he could meet those challenges.

Roberts was a progressive man. At a time when a woman was considered adequately educated who had the basic rudiments of arithmetic and reading and a knowledge of homemaking, he was diligently searching for schools which would challenge the minds of his daughters. He hoped to pass on to his children his love of books. His three hundred volume library and the special closet built to house the books points to an unusually active mind, especially at a time when the usual family was considered lucky to own one book—the Bible.

For the time in which he lived, Roberts was a wealthy man. In addition to lands worth sixteen thousand dollars on the tax rolls (probably much more in the marketplace), he owned a beautiful residence, a barn and outbuildings, a saw mill, sheep, cattle and appropriate farm machinery. He owned one hundred sixty shares of railroad stock and enough cash to leave over thirty thousand dollars.

When we think of Roberts, the words intellectual, conscientious, quiet, handsome, serious, and sober come to mind. The picture of Roberts laughing uproariously at some bawdy story is not in keeping with the man. Life was a serious business.

The last ten years of Roberts' life were a drastic change from his life of the previous twenty. With no more canals to build, his life became that of a gentleman farmer. He seemed to accept the role philosophically if not joyfully, busying himself with matters at hand. There were high points such as his appointment to the Constitutional Convention and his appointment as a side judge in the Court of Common Pleas.

In spite of Roberts' obvious successes, he remains an enigma. References to him are almost non-existent. Although he was responsible for the establishment of the village of Canastota, the people of the village do not know his name, nor is he mentioned in either of the two histories of Madison County nor in accounts of the famous men of the county. It is true that he was away from home for long periods of time making it impossible for him to participate in the politics of the county. Also his home was not in the village proper; however, when he was at home, he was a devoted churchgoer and a community-minded citizen. His wife and children always lived at the residence and judging from the crowd at Mary Jane's funeral, were popular.

Roberts was a quiet person, but he had the poise to associate with and to be a friend to Governor Bouck. Perhaps the natives of Canastota found him forbidding since he found little time for village small talk. He was certainly not the hail-fellow-well-met type and so might have been considered a snob with his wealth and national reputation in canal circles. In addition, he was a liberal Democrat in a conservative Republican area. Perhaps it is as simple as the old saying: "A prophet is without honor in his own country." However, it must be noted that when one looks at a map or early canal building in America, the stamp of Nathan Roberts may be found on each one.

Bibliography

Andrist, Ralph K., *The Erie Canal.* New York: the American Heritage Publishing Company (1964): pp. 34-35, 44-45.

Barlow, Eugene, "Autographs of Prominent Men of Madison County." Speech given to the Madison County Historical Society, 1908.

Bouck, William C., "Bouck Papers." # 226, Cornell University Libraries, Dept. of Manuscripts and University Archives, Ithaca, N.Y.

Canastota Bee Journal, Saturday, February 7, 1906. "Memoirs of Nathan S. Roberts, Personal Reminiscences," pp. 3, 7-9, 11-12, 16-18, 21, 24-26, 28-29, 31, 35, 42-45, 47-50, 53-54, 56-57.

Colden, pp. 14, 16-17.

Columbia Encyclopedia, 3rd edition (1963). Columbia University Press, New York: p. 1442.

Congdon, George E., *Stars in the Water*, Garden City, N.Y.: Doubleday and Company (1974): pp. 13, 15, 19, 26, 28, 41, 56-57, 69-70, 86-91, 205, 220-222.

Drago, Harry S., *Canal Days in America.* New York: Clarkson N. Potter (1972): pp. 32-33, 47-73, 143, 145, 165, 184-192.

Fitzsimmons, pp. 26-28, 31, 34.

Galpin, W. Freeman, Syracuse University: *The Pioneer Days.* Syracuse, N.Y., Syracuse University Press (1952: pp. 112-114.

———, *Central New York.* New York: Lewis Historical Pub. Co., Inc. (1941): pp. 208-209.

Goodrich, Bert, ed. *Madison County Heritage.* Oneida, N.Y.: Madison County Historical Society, September 1979.

Harlowe, Alvin, *Old Towpath.* Port Washington, N.Y.: Kennikat Press, Inc. (1964): pp. 46, 60, 66, 68-74, 71, 93, 95-98, 100-105, 223-226.

Hosack, David, *Memoir of Dewitt Clinton.* New York: Heritage Publishing Company (1829): pp. 34, 35, 44, 45, 85.

Memorials of Elder John White one of the first settlers of Hartford, Connecticut and of his descendants, by Allyn S. Kellogg. Hartford: Printed for the family by Case, Lockwood and Co., 1860.

"Paintings of Grove S. Gilbert," Rochester Historical Society, XIV, 1936: pp. 54-60.

Peck, W.F., *Rochester and Monroe Co.*, 3 vols. Pioneer Pub. Co. (1884): Vol. 1, p. 52.

Rome Historical Society, newspaper clippings. Folder 2126.

Smith, Walter W., ed. "Diary of Nathan Roberts, Civil Engineer for the Erie Canal." unpublished ms., pp 1-6, 9, 11, 17, 19.

Stuart, Charles B., *Lives and Work of Military Engineers of America*. New York: D. Van Nostrand, Publishing (1871): pp. 109-110, 112-113.

"The Village History," *The Evening Courant*, Canastota, N.Y., August 21, 1902.

Wager, Daniel E., ed. *Oneida County.* Boston Historic Company (1896): pp. 86-87.

Will of Nathan Roberts. Madison County Surrogate's Office, Madison County Court House, Wampsville, N.Y.

Will of Lavania Roberts. Madison County Surrogate's Office, Madison County Court House, Wampsville, N.Y.